Addison Peale Russell

In a Club Corner

The Monologue of a Man who might have been Sociable

Addison Peale Russell
In a Club Corner
The Monologue of a Man who might have been Sociable
ISBN/EAN: 9783743328341

Manufactured in Europe, USA, Canada, Australia, Japa

Cover: Foto ©ninafisch / pixelio.de

Manufactured and distributed by brebook publishing software (www.brebook.com)

Addison Peale Russell

In a Club Corner

In a Club Corner

THE MONOLOGUE OF A MAN WHO MIGHT
HAVE BEEN SOCIABLE

OVERHEARD BY

A. P. RUSSELL

AUTHOR OF "A CLUB OF ONE," "LIBRARY NOTES," "CHARACTER-
ISTICS," ETC.

BOSTON AND NEW YORK
HOUGHTON, MIFFLIN AND COMPANY
The Riverside Press, Cambridge
1890

CONTENTS

	PAGE
Conversation	7
Originality	39
One Quality of the Great	46
Precept and Practice	51
Long Sermons	56
Old Age	57
Oblivion	81
Subsisting by Authorship	84
Pretension	89
Shakespeare	92
Paradoxes	96
Solitude	107
Style	110
Public Speaking	114
Books and Reading	119
Vanity	129
Justice and Mercy	132
Sheridan	137
Garrick	152
On Giving Advice	164
Limits	166
On Working Ourselves Up	168
Of Incalculable Forces	171

Contents

Deceiving through the Affections	176
A Pretty Legend	177
Selecting Memories	178
Manners	192
Self-Portraiture	197
The Philosopher's Stone	198
Reading Aloud	202
The Oblique Tendency	210
Whistling	214
Sentimentalism	215
Cost of Excellence	219
Youth and Age	226
Schools of Morals	229
Chairs of Common Sense	229
Small Things	230
Sects and Creeds	238
Good out of Evil	239
The Faith Cure	241
Poverty	243
Digestion	251
Heroism	253
Character	255
The Hope	267
Intuition and Worship	274
Friendship	278
Ignorance	279
Faces	279
Heredity	288
The Laconic	296

Contents

Monotony and Familiarity	302
Sleep of the Mind	304
The Friendly Guidance of Necessity	308
The Palm of Destiny	309
Content	314
Democracy	316
Proud Possessors	318
Responsibility	320
Essays in Titles	321

IN A CLUB CORNER

N Dean Swift's Hints towards an Essay on Conversation, he sets out by saying that he had observed few obvious subjects to have been so seldom, or at least so slightly, handled as this, and that few were so difficult to treat. Conversation is an art, says Emerson, in which a man has all mankind for his competitors, for it is that which all are practicing every day while they live. Metternich is reported to have said, "In my whole life I have only known ten or twelve persons with whom it is pleasant to speak—that is, who keep to the subject, do not repeat themselves, and do not talk of themselves; men who do not listen to their own voices, who are cultivated not to lose themselves in commonplaces; and lastly, who possess tact and good sense enough not to elevate their own persons above their subjects." Steele said, "It is a secret known but to

Conversation.

Metternich's experience.

few, yet of no small use in the conduct of life, that when you fall into a man's conversation, the first thing that you should consider is, whether he has a greater inclination to hear you, or that you should hear him." "To please," observed Chamfort, "one must make up his mind to be taught many things which he already knows, by people who do not know them." "The reason why few persons are agreeable in conversation," thought La Rochefoucauld, "is because each thinks more of what he intends to say than of what others are saying, and seldom listens but when he desires to speak." La Bruyère was of opinion that "the art of conversation consists much less in your own abundance than in enabling others to find talk for themselves. Men do not wish to admire you; they want to please. The wit of conversation consists more in finding it in others than in showing a great deal yourself; he who goes from your conversation pleased with himself and his own wit is perfectly well pleased with you."

The first thing to consider.

In what the wit of conversation mainly consists.

The question was once put to Aristotle, how we ought to behave to our friends, and the answer he gave was, "As we should wish our friends to behave to us." The world has been justly likened to a looking-glass, which gives back to every man the reflection of his own face. Frown at it, and it will in turn look sourly upon you; laugh at it and with it, and it is a jolly, kind companion.

One of the best rules in conversation, in the opinion of Swift, is never to say a thing which any of the company can reasonably wish we had left unsaid; nor can anything be well more contrary to the ends for which people meet together than to part unsatisfied with each other or themselves. Conversation, in the judgment of Sydney Smith, must and ought to grow out of materials on which men can agree, not upon subjects which try the passions. *A rule of Swift's.*

Lady Mary Wortley Montagu, who had tried all things, pronounced a chosen conversation, composed of a few that one esteems, the greatest happiness of life. Of indoor entertainment, it has been remarked, the truest and most humane is that of conversation. But this social amusement is not, in all circumstances, to be got, and when it is to be had, we are not always fit for it. The art of conversation is so little cultivated, the tongue is so little refined, the play of wit and the *The greatest happiness of life.*

flow of fancy are so little encouraged or esteemed, that our social gatherings are too often stupid and wearisome. Talkative men, it has been observed, seldom read. This is among the few truths which appear the more strange the more we reflect upon them? For what is reading but silent conversation? Conversation, said Sterne, is a traffic; and if you enter into it without some stock of knowledge to balance the account perpetually betwixt you, the trade drops at once. Though, as Dr. Holmes has said, "Nobody talks much that does n't say unwise things, — things he did not mean to say; as no person plays much without striking a false note sometimes. Talk, to me, is only spading up the ground for crops of thought. I can't answer for what will turn up. If I could, it would n't be talking, but 'speaking my piece.' Better, I think, the hearty abandonment of one's self to the suggestions of the moment, at the risk of an occasional slip of the tongue, perceived the instant it escapes, but just one syllable too late, than the royal reputation of never saying a foolish thing." Alcott expressed the belief that "in conversation fine things may be said, but the best must come of themselves;

Talkative men seldom read.

Abandonment of one's self.

they cannot be coerced; they must be born of the soul. All true conversation is spontaneous, and only comes when the gods are near. When the gods are distant it is because of adverse influences. The intuitions are the essence of all wisdom, and all the intuitions come from the shrine of nature, which we must hold in reverence. There is no finite. The circles of our being begin and end in eternity."

True conversation spontaneous.

A great good of conversation is, that it fills all gaps, supplies all deficiencies, and makes you forgetful of particulars. It is recorded of Madame de Maintenon that, during dinner, the servant slipped to her side, "Please, madame, one anecdote more, for there is no roast to-day." Who does not remember occasions when the feast was the least part of the entertainment? when the flavor of the delicate and rich dishes was lost in the higher satisfaction of the intellectual palate?

Madame de Maintenon.

The foundation of all good conversation is what the poet Rowe pronounces the foundation of all the virtues — good nature: "which is friendship between man and man; good breeding in courts; charity in religion; and the true spring of all beneficence in general." Censoriousness is almost sure to have its origin in ill-nature or self-reproach. In such case those who indulge in it (to quote Lady Blessington) "consider the severity of their censures on the failings of others as an atonement for their own."

Censoriousness.

It is well to remember the saying, that nature has created man with two ears and but one tongue. "I did not hear what you said," ejaculated an exuberant talker, by way of contradiction. "I don't know how you should have heard it," was the reply, "for you never hear anything." "I am very fond of society," said Madame du Deffand; "all the world listens to me, and I listen to nobody." Liszt is reported as saying of George Eliot: "Ugly though she was, Miss Evans had a charm, and knew how to captivate those around her." At times her way of listening reminded him of George Sand. She seemed to absorb like a sponge everything she saw and heard. Her long, ill-favored face put on an expression of attention so rapt that it became positively interesting. George Sand, he said, caught her butterfly and tamed it in her box by giving it grass and flowers — this was the love period. Then she stuck her pin into it when it struggled

George Eliot and George Sand.

— this was the congé, and it always came from her. Afterward she vivisected it, stuffed it, and added it to her collection of heroes for novels. It was this traffic of souls which had given themselves up unreservedly to her which eventually disgusted him with her. By the faculty of attentively listening to what others had to say, Madame Roland affirms that she made more friends than by any remarks she ever made of her own. Judicious silence is one of the great social virtues. Quaint old Burton tells of a woman who, hearing one of the gossips by chance complain of her husband's impatience, told her an excellent remedy for it, and gave her withal a glass of water, which when he brawled she should hold still in her mouth, and that toties quoties, as often as he chid: she did so twice or three times with good success, and at length, seeing her neighbor, gave her great thanks for it, and would needs know the ingredients: she told her in brief what it was; fair water, and no more; for it was not the water, but her silence which performed the cure. *Madame Roland.* *Silence the remedy.*

Those who have been renowned for their powers of conversation were constantly exercising them. Addison would pass seven or eight hours a day in coffee-houses and taverns. Johnson told Boswell that his habit was to go out at four o'clock in the afternoon and not to return till two in the morning. A great time for these great men to spend in talk. Lady Mary Wortley Montagu declared Addison was the best company in the world; and Pope confessed that his great compeer's conversation had something in it more charming than he had found in any other man. "But this," the poet said, "was only when familiar: before strangers, or perhaps a single stranger, he preserved his dignity by a stiff silence." It is stated that whenever Boswell came into a company where Horace Walpole was, Walpole would throw back his head, purse up his mouth very significantly, and not speak a word while Boswell remained.

Addison.

Walpole.

The wits of Horace Walpole's day, Sir George Selwyn, Sir Hanbury Williams, Bubb Doddington, Charles Townshend, and their associates, it is difficult to judge of at the distance of more than a century from their times. But it would appear their wit was of the social, unpremeditated, conversational character, in which Sydney Smith, Talleyrand, Hook, and Barham particularly excelled. Sydney Smith, it is *Sydney Smith.* known, could not make the smallest remark without provoking a laugh; and even when he said grace, the young lady who sat next to him said, "You always are so amusing." His compliment to Lady D. is worth remembering. "She seems," he said, "to be a very sensible and very worthy person. I must do her the justice to say that when my jokes are explained to her, and she has leisure to reflect upon them, she laughs very heartily."

Everybody has heard of Hook's famous *Hook.* reply when, after having returned from the colonies, where he was in an official position, under suspicion of peculation, a friend meeting him said, "Why, hello, Hook! I did not know you were in England. What has brought you back again?" "Something wrong about the chest," replied the imperturbable wit.

It has been remarked upon as singular that one known to have been habitually as silent as Talleyrand should have left a *Talleyrand.* reputation for brilliancy in the social circle. From his habit of nearly closing his eyes — a habit that grew upon him as he advanced in years — he could scarcely have appeared even an attentive or interested listener.

His drooped eyelids, and the smile on his face, would rather seemingly have indicated a mind occupied with some dreamy thoughts of his own. Yet, when, occasionally, half rising from his seat, or changing his position, he opened his eyes on the company, with a glance full of malice, but not of ill-nature, and uttered some piquant remark or amusing bon mot (which he had, doubtless, been meditating), he gave, in a few words, a concentrated reply, as it were, to the whole conversation. And usually it was so fit, so appropriate, that it fixed itself in the memory of his hearers; unlike the wordy declamation which, as a noise in the air, floated away from Madame de Staël's admiring audience, without leaving a trace of its meaning in the mind.

Malicious but not ill-natured.

Lord Brougham, who speaks from a personal and delightful intimacy, eulogizes Talleyrand's conversation: "Of his truly inimitable conversation, and the mixture of strong masculine sense, and exquisitely witty turns in which it abounds — independently of the interest, and the solid value which it derived from a rich fund of anecdote, delivered in the smallest number possible of the most happy and most appropriate words possible, it would indeed

Brougham's eulogy.

be difficult to convey an adequate idea. His own powers of picturesque, and wonderfully condensed expression, would be hardly sufficient to present a portrait of its various and striking beauties. Simple and natural, yet abounding in the most sudden and unexpected turns; full of point, yet evidently the inspiration of the moment, and therefore more absolutely to the purpose than if they had been the labored effort of a day's reflection — a single word often performing the office of sentences, nay, a tone not unfrequently rendering many words superfluous — always the phrase most perfectly suitable selected, and its place most happily chosen — all this is literally correct, and no picture of fancy, but a mere abridgment and transcript of the marvelous original; yet it falls very short of conveying its lineaments, and fails still more to render its coloring and its shades. For there was a constant gayety of manner which had the mirthful aspect of good-humor, even on the eve or on the morrow of some flash in which his witty raillery had wrapped a subject or a person in ridicule, or of some torrent in which his satire had descended instantaneous but destructive; there was an archness of

Condensed expression.

Gayety of manner.

malice when more than ordinary execution must be done, that defied the pencil of the describer, as it did the attempts of the imitator; there were manners the most perfect in ease, in grace, in flexibility; there was the voice of singular depth and modulation, and the countenance alike fitted to express earnest respect, unostentatious contempt, and bland complacency; and all this must have been really witnessed to be accurately understood."

His circumspection. "His circumspection," said Napoleon, "was extreme. He treated his friends as if they might, in future, become his enemies, and he behaved to his enemies as if they might, some time or other, become his friends. Mademoiselle Raucourt, a celebrated actress, described him with great truth. 'If you ask him a question,' said she, 'he is an iron chest, whence you cannot extract a syllable; but if you ask him nothing, you will soon be unable to stop his mouth, he will become a regular gossip.' *His countenance.* The countenance of Talleyrand is so immovable that nothing can be read in it. Lannes and Murat used jocularly to say of him, that if while he was speaking to you, some one should come behind and give him a kick, his countenance would betray nothing."

Macaulay met Talleyrand at Holland House, and had the pleasure of listening for an hour and a half to his conversation. The great Frenchman was then an old man. "He is certainly," said Macaulay, in a letter to his sister, "the greatest curiosity that I ever fell in with. His head is sunk down between two high shoulders. One of his feet is hideously distorted. His face is as pale as that of a corpse, and wrinkled to a frightful degree. His eyes have an odd glassy stare quite peculiar to them. His hair, thickly powdered and pomatumed, hangs down his shoulders on each side as straight as a pound of tallow candles. His conversation, however, soon makes you forget his ugliness and infirmities. There is a poignancy without effort in all that he says, which reminded me a little of the character which the wits of Johnson's circle give of Beauclerk. He told several stories about the political men of France: not of any great value in themselves: but his way of telling them was beyond all praise; concise, pointed, and delicately satirical."

Coleridge was one of those enthusiasts whose minds are absorbed by the doctrines they have last espoused. Southey de-

His habit of repeating himself.

scribes him as repeating the same thing to every fresh company; and if they were at seven parties in the week, his set speech was delivered seven times. His pauses occurred at intervals of about a quarter of an hour, and he did not suffer the second personage in the dialogue to thrust in more than a few hasty words before he launched anew upon his loquacious discourse.

Two persons, Underwood and McKenzie, who had many opportunities of observing Coleridge, are reported by Dilke (long the editor of the London Athenæum, and the personal friend of Keats, Lamb, Procter, etc.) to have arrived at the conclusion that there was more humbug in Coleridge than in any man that was ever heard of. Underwood was one day transcribing something for Coleridge, when a visitor appeared. After the commonplaces, Coleridge took up a little book lying upon the

Manner described.

table, and said, "By-the-bye, I casually took up this little book this morning, and was quite enchanted with a little sonnet I found there." He then read off a blank verse translation, and entered into a long critique upon its merits. The same story, the same translation, the same critique, were repeated five times in that day to different visitors, without one word being altered. Mr. Underwood said that every one of his famous winning conversations was got up. This habit of repetition was not confined to his conversation. In every one of his writings, says his nephew, there are repetitions, either literal or substantial, of passages to be found in some others of those writings; and there are several particular positions and reasonings which he considered of vital importance, reiterated in the Friend, the Literary Life, the Lay Sermons, the Aids to Reflection, and the Church and State. He was always deepening and widening the foundation, and cared not how often he used the same stone. *Conversations got up.*

In illustration of Coleridge's unfailing talk, Procter gives an account of one of his days, when he was present. He had come from Highgate to London, for the sole purpose of consulting a friend about his son Hartley ("our dear Hartley"), for whom he expressed, and no doubt felt, much anxiety. He arrived about one or two o'clock, in the midst of a conversation which immediately began to interest him. He struck into the middle of the talk very soon, and "held the ear of the house" until dinner made its appearance about *Procter's account.*

Talked without interruption.

four o'clock. He then talked all through the dinner, all the afternoon, all the evening, with scarcely a single interruption. He expatiated on this subject and on that; he drew fine distinctions; he made subtle criticisms. He descended to anecdotes, critical, logical, historical; he dealt with law, medicine, and divinity, until at last, five minutes before eight o'clock, the servant came in and announced that the Highgate stage was at the corner of the street, and was waiting to convey Mr. Coleridge home. Coleridge immediately started up, oblivious of all time, and said, in a hurried voice, "My dear F——, I will come to you some other day, and talk to you about our dear Hartley." He had quite forgotten his son and everybody else, in the delight of having such an enraptured audience.

His preaching tone.

His preaching tone is well-known, and has often been described. Lamb and Coleridge were once talking together on the incidents of Coleridge's early life, when he was beginning his career in the Church, and Coleridge was describing some of the facts in his usual tone, when he paused, and said: "Pray, Mr. Lamb, did you ever hear me preach?" "Damme," said Lamb, "I never heard you do anything else."

Wordsworth was to breakfast with Procter one morning, but being much after the appointed time, he excused himself by stating that he and a friend had been to see Coleridge, who had detained them by one continuous flow of talk. "How was it you called so early?" inquired Rogers. "Oh!" said Wordsworth, "we are going to dine with him this evening, and"— "And," said Rogers, taking up the sentence, "you wanted to take 'the sting' out of him beforehand." *Wordsworth's excuse.*

Macaulay was met by Crabb Robinson at a dinner-party, about the time the former began to be famous. The barrister describes him in his diary as "very eloquent and cheerful. Overflowing with words, and not poor in thought. He seems a correct as well as a full man. He showed a minute knowledge of subjects not introduced by himself." He was a favorite at Holland House. Lady Holland, we are told, listened to him with unwonted deference, and scolded him with a circumspection that was in itself a compliment. Rogers spoke of him with friendliness, and to him with positive affection. Sharp treated him with great kindness and consideration. For the space of three seasons *Macaulay.* *A compliment.*

he dined out almost nightly, and spent many of his Sundays in the suburban mansions of his friends. Lord Carlisle, in his journal, mentions having met Macaulay at a dinner. "Never," he says, "were such *Torrents of* torrents of good talk as burst and sputtered over from Macaulay and Hallam." He refers also to a breakfast with Macaulay in his rooms at the top of the Albany — their walls covered with seven to ten thousand books. Macaulay's conversation, he says, "ranged the world." "To remember his talk," says Thackeray, "is to wonder: to think not only of the treasures he had in his memory, but of the trifles he had stored there, and could produce with equal readiness. Every man who has known *Thackeray's* him has his story regarding that astonishing memory. It may be that he was not ill-pleased that you should recognize it; but to those prodigious intellectual feats, which were so easy to him, who would grudge his tribute of homage?"

What he said of Churchill was perhaps applicable to himself, — "There was too great a tendency to say with willing vehemence whatever could be eloquently said:" he must needs, it seems, be ever talking or writing somebody or something up or down. Hayward said, "Give Lord Macaulay a hint, a fancy, an insulated fact or phrase, a scrap of a journal, or the tag end of a song, and on it, by the abused prerogative of genius, he would construct a theory of national or personal character, which should confer undying glory or inflict indelible disgrace." *Hayward's criticism.*

From all accounts, there must have been a good deal of the declamatory, the aggressive, the irrepressible, the overwhelming in the manner and conversation of Madame de Staël. Byron said she ought to have been a man. Heine called her "a hurricane in a petticoat." No wonder Napoleon hated her and hunted her. She did consent to be silent, to wait, to suffer the loss of all things dear to her ; but she refused a word of homage to power. The Minister of Police (Fouché) demanded only the insertion of a flattery in Corinne. She answered that she was ready to take out of it anything offensive, but not to add anything to make her court to the government. *Madame de Staël.*

"She was born to be a damper, this young woman!" exclaimed Gabriel Varden of Miggs, his old servant (in Barnaby Rudge). In the souvenirs of Madame le Brun she recites that, while traveling in *A damper.*

Madame le Brun's extinguisher.

a carriage in Italy with a gentleman whom circumstances brought in her way, she had the following experience: "As we were crossing the Pontine marshes I perceived a shepherd seated on the bank of a canal, whilst his sheep browsed in a field carpeted with flowers, beyond which one could see the sea and Cape Circée. 'This would make a charming picture,' I said to my companion—'the shepherd, the sheep, *The sheep all dirty.* the prairie, and the sea.' 'These sheep are all dirty,' he replied; 'you should see the English sheep.' Again, on the road to Tenadna, I saw on the left the line of the Apennines surrounded by superb clouds that the setting sun had lightened; I could not refrain from expressing my *The superb clouds only promising rain.* admiration. 'These clouds only promise us rain to-morrow,' said my companion." Farther along on the journey, she adds: "The road to Naples is charming; here and there beautiful trees are seen, and the hedges are masses of wild roses and scented myrtles. I was enchanted, though my companion said he preferred the sunny, fine slopes of Bordeaux, which promised good wine." Madame le Brun called this gentleman her "extinguisher," and soon had the satisfaction of saying good-by to him.

In Gil Blas is an allusion to a dozen people sitting at supper. It was whimsical enough: the whole party plied their knives and forks without speaking a word, except one man, who talked incessantly, right or wrong, and made up for the silence of the rest by his eternal babble. He affected to be a wit, to tell a good story, and took great pains to make the good folks merry by his puns; and accordingly they did laugh most inextinguishably; but it was at him, not with him. *A scene from Gil Blas.*

"If you are ever at a loss to support a flagging conversation," says Leigh Hunt, "introduce the subject of eating." No man is ignorant or reticent on that interesting subject. Nor does he fail to be intelligent and loquacious when his neighbors are to be discussed. Those persons, it has been said, who from folly or from carelessness tell one friend what another friend says of him would do well to consider the observation, true or not, of the acute and amiable Pascal: "All men naturally hate each other. I am certain that if they were to know accurately what they occasionally had said of one another, there would not be four persons in the world who could long preserve their friendship for one another." *The subject of eating.*

An observation of Pascal.

Conversation in sick-rooms.

As to too much of the conversation in sick-rooms, Dr. Holmes in his Autocrat remarks: "As you go down the social scale, you reach a point at length where the common talk in sick-rooms is of churchyards and sepulchres, and a kind of perpetual vivisection is forever carried on upon the person of the miserable sufferer."

The same witty and wise genius, in the Poet at the Breakfast-Table, says: "People you talk with every day have got to *Feeders for the mind.* have feeders for their minds, as much as the stream that turns a mill-wheel has. It isn't one little rill that's going to keep the float boards turning round. Take a dozen of the brightest men you can find in the brightest city, wherever that may be, and let 'em come together once a month, and you'll find out in the course of a year or two the ones that have feeders from all the hillsides. Your common talkers, that exchange the gossip of the day, have no wheel *Wash of the street.* in particular to turn, and the wash of the rain as it runs down the street is enough for them."

Truly it is said that, cultivate as you will, decree as you will, begild with titles, overload with privileges and possessions, there is among men but one genuine superiority, the superiority of mind, — a *Superiority of mind.* superiority resulting from the union of the higher intellect with the higher feelings. "Through life," says Thackeray, "Swift, somehow, seems always to be alone. Goethe was so. I can't fancy Shakespeare otherwise. The giants must live apart. The kings can have no company. . . . Looking at the calm, fair face and clear countenance of Addison, — those chiseled features pure and cold, — I can't but fancy that this great man was also one of the lonely ones of the world. Such men have *The lonely ones of the* very few equals, and they don't herd with *world.* those. It is in the nature of such lords of intellect to be solitary — they are in the world, but not of it; and our minor struggles, brawls, successes, pass under them." It always seemed to Holmes as if Emerson looked upon this earth very much as a visitor from another planet would look on it. He was interested, and to some extent curious about it, but it was not the first spheroid he had been acquainted with, by any means. Richter has said, the more powerful and intellectual and great two men are, so much the less can they bear each other under one ceiling, as great insects, which live on fruits, are unsocial (for example, in every hazel-nut there sits only one chafer), whereas the little ones, which live only on leaves, — for instance, the leaf-lice, — cleave together inseparably.

Burns.

Some one said of Burns, "He is great in verse, greater in prose, still greater in conversation." Eminent people, like Robertson the historian, ladies of rank, like the Duchess of Gordon, and the servants at the inns, who, if Burns came in late, would "get out of bed to hear him talk," testify to his powers. We have an account of a call that two Englishmen made upon him. They found him fishing. He received them with cordiality, and asked them to share his humble dinner. He was in his happiest mood, and the charm of his conversation was altogether fascinating. He ranged over a variety of topics, illuminating whatever he touched. He related the tales of his infancy and youth; he recited some of his gayest and some of his tenderest poems; in the wildest of the strains of his mirth he threw in some touches of melancholy, and spread around him the electric emotions of his powerful nature. The Highland whiskey improved in its flavor; the marble bowl was again and again emptied and replenished; the guests

A dinner with the poet.

of the poet forgot the flight of time and the dictates of prudence; at the hour of midnight they lost their way to Dumfries, and could scarcely distinguish it when assisted by the morning's dawn.

"Madame Recamier," said De Tocqueville (in conversation with Mr. Senior), "was the delight of Paris, but she said very little. She listened and smiled intelligently, and from time to time threw in a question or a remark to show that she understood you. From long habit she knew what were the subjects on which each guest showed to most advantage, and she put him upon them. The last, indeed, was not difficult, for the guest knew better even than she did his forte, and seized the thread that led to it. It was only by inference, only by inquiring why it was that one talked more easily at her house than elsewhere, that one discovered the perfection of her art." At another time he said to Mr. Senior, "I knew well Madame Recamier. Few traces of her former beauty remained; but we were all her lovers and her slaves. The talent, labor, and skill, which she wasted on her salon, would have gained and governed an empire. She was virtuous, if it be virtuous to persuade every

Madame Recamier.

Her lovers and slaves.

one of a dozen men to believe that you wish to favor him, though some circumstances always seemed to prevent your doing so. Every friend thought himself preferred. She governed us by little distinctions, by letting one man come five minutes before the others, or stay five minutes after, just as Louis XIV. raised one courtier to the seventh heaven by giving him the taper at night, and another by taking his shirt from him in the morning. As I have remarked, the Madame said little, but knew what each man's forte was, and placed from time to time a mot which led him to it. If anything were peculiarly well said, her face brightened. You saw that her attention was always active and always intelligent."

Little distinctions.

Mathews. Charles Mathews, the elder, must have been a delightful conversationalist in his way. Perhaps no one ever existed who carried more genius into his jesting. Everything and everybody seemed imitable by him. What a dinner that must have been where Scott and Byron and Mathews sat down together — an occasion and event of so much importance as to have been specially noted by each one of them. Lockhart says that Sir Walter recorded it in his note-book as "the most interesting day he ever spent." The great actor's ruling tendency was conspicuous throughout the whole of his life. It is said that the attendant in his last illness intended to give his patient some medicine; but a few moments afterward it was discovered that the medicine was nothing but ink, which had been taken from the vial by mistake, and his friend exclaimed, "Good Heavens, Mathews, I have given you ink!" "Never mind, my boy," said Mathews, faintly; "I'll swallow a bit of blotting-paper."

Ruling tendency.

Diplomatists are thought to be dissemblers, though sometimes very remarkable for their frankness. Count Cavour and Prince Bismarck may be cited as instances. Once when the Prussian envoy at Turin, astonished at Cavour's freedom of speech, was searching for some hidden meaning in his words, Cavour replied quickly, "Do not deceive yourself. I say only what I think. As for the habit attributed to diplomatists of disguising their thoughts, it is one of which I never avail myself." He used often to say laughingly to his friends, "Now I have found out the art of deceiving diplomatists: I speak the truth, and I am certain they will not believe me."

Cavour and Bismarck.

Carlyle. Thirty odd years ago, Carlyle, as a social power, or a social plague, was already troubling the still surface of London drawing-room life. "What is his talk like?" asked Miss Berry of her friend; and Kinglake answered, "Ezekiel." Thackeray said, "The man is a bully, but he can be silenced by persiflage;" a remark that is interesting in connection with Carlyle's recorded verdict of Thackeray.

Scott. Scott was a fine humorist in conversation. Irving has preserved a good specimen of his talk. One morning at breakfast, when Dominie Thomson, the tutor, was present, Scott was going on with great glee to relate an anecdote of the Laird of Macnab, "who, poor fellow," premised he, "is dead and gone." "Why, Mr. Scott," exclaimed his lady, "Macnab's not dead, is he?" "Faith, my dear," replied Scott, with humorous gravity, "if he's not dead, they have done him great injustice, for they've buried him." The joke passed harmless and unnoticed by Mrs. Scott, but hit the poor Dominie just as he had raised a cup of tea to his lips, causing a burst of laughter which sent half of the contents about the table. Hogg said that Scott's anecdotes were without end; he was almost certain they were all made off-hand, as he never heard one of them either before or after.

Lamb was present at a party of North Britons, where a son of Burns was expected, and happened to drop a "silly expression" (in his South British way), that he wished it were the father instead of the son, — when four of them started up at once to inform him that "that was impossible, because he was dead." An impracticable wish was more than they could conceive. *Lamb.*

"What sort of a man was Douglas Jerrold?" was asked of Mr. Addey, an old London publisher. "He was a little man," was the reply, "about five feet high, long hair, prominent cheek-bones, a keen eye, and his form a little bent, and he looked up at you with a comical wag of his head. I knew him very well. He was really kind-hearted and sympathetic, but he was so fond of fun and so sarcastic in his method that he sometimes indulged his wit at the expense of other people's feelings. Not many got ahead of him. His publishers, Bradbury & Evans, who, he thought, had treated him rather shabbily, gave him a couple of sucking pigs, which he took out *Douglas Jerrold.*

to his suburban cottage, and put in a pen. He named them, one Bradbury and the other Evans. A couple of months after that, his publishers came out and dined with him. After dinner he took them out and showed them his pigs, and said, 'I have named them after you, gentlemen. They are growing wonderfully, and I believe if I keep them they will grow the greatest hogs in Europe, and I do not forget the donors.' Jerrold's conversation sparkled with epigrams, and no man ever laughed more heartily at his own jokes. If you heard Douglas Jerrold roaring with delight and holding his sides, you immediately inferred that he had said something. His laugh was unaffected, and very contagious. Like all literary men, he was never half paid." He told Addey that for his great comedy of Black-Eyed Susan, which still holds possession of the stage, he received just what Milton did for his Paradise Lost — twenty-five dollars — and the publisher made fifteen thousand from it the first year.

"Call that a kind man?" said an actor, speaking of an acquaintance; "a man who is away from his family and never sends them a farthing? Call that kindness?"

Marginalia: Jerrold's pigs. Black-Eyed Susan.

"Yes; unremitting," replied Jerrold. Speaking of patriotism, he said, "When a man has nothing in the world to lose, he is then in the best condition to sacrifice for the public good everything that is his." "They say," he said, "a parson first invented gunpowder, but one cannot believe it till one is married."

Unremitting kindness.

There is a story of Moore asking Rogers what he did when people who wanted his autograph requested him to sign a sentence. "Oh, I give them, 'Ill-gotten wealth never prospers,' or 'Virtue is its own reward.'" "Then the more shame for you," Luttrell broke in, "to circulate such delusions."

The wit of Dumas has been pronounced as near as any earthly thing may be to the wit of heaven, which, by the inimitable Sydney Smith, was called lightning. The story of his parentage is well known. A certain coxcomb, wishing to mortify the great dramatist, asked him point-blank who was his father. "A mulatto, sir," coldly replied Dumas, imperceptibly divining the intended insult. "And your grandfather?" "A negro, sir." "And your great-grandfather?" "A baboon, sir!" thundered Dumas at his now terrified questioner; "a

The wit of Dumas.

baboon, sir! My ancestry begins where yours ends." Wit of this sort strikes and scathes like the lightning. It bites and crushes like a vise. Sugden hated Brougham, and took his revenge in the famous bon mot, that it was a pity he did not know a little law, and then he would have a smattering of everything. Lord Thurlow was storming one day at his old valet, who thought little of a violence with which he had been long familiar, and "Go to the devil, do!" cried the enraged master; "Go, I say, to the devil." "Give me a character, my Lord," replied the fellow, dryly; "people like, you know, to have characters from their acquaintances." Curran, being asked what an Irish gentleman, just arrived in England, could mean by perpetually putting out his tongue, answered, "I suppose he's trying to catch the English accent." In his last illness, his physician observing in the morning that he seemed to cough with more difficulty, he answered, "That is rather surprising, as I have been practicing all night."

Rogers was unceasingly at war with Lady Davy. One day at dinner she called across the table, "Now, Mr. Rogers, I am sure you are talking about me."

.

"Lady Davy," was the retort, "I pass my life in defending you." The plea which he advanced for his bitterness was, in itself, a satire. "They tell me I say ill-natured things," he observed, in his slow, quiet, deliberate way. "I have a very weak voice; if I did not say ill-natured things, no one would hear what I said." He told of an Englishman and a Frenchman who had to fight a duel. That they might have the better chance of missing one another, they were to fight in a dark room. The Englishman fired up the chimney, and brought down the Frenchman! "When I tell this story in Paris," observed Rogers, "I put the Englishman up the chimney."

A plea for bitterness.

Every one at all familiar with the writings of Lord Macaulay remembers the oft-repeated sentence in his famous tribute to the Catholic Church: "And she may still exist in undiminished vigor when some traveler from New Zealand shall, in the midst of a vast solitude, take his stand on a broken arch of London Bridge to sketch the ruins of St. Paul's." In one of Horace Walpole's letters to Sir Horace Mann, written half a century or more before, may be found this similar sentence: "At last,

ORIGINALITY.

Macaulay's New Zealander.

some curious traveler from Lima will visit England, and give a description of the ruins of St. Paul's, like the editions of Baalbec and Palmyra." Every reader should be familiar with that most remarkable story of patriotism, A Man without a Country. Madame de Genlis in her Memoirs refers to the work of M. de Ballange, entitled The Man without a Name, in which the author painted with the most terrible energy all the horrors of remorse for a fearful crime. "There are ideas," says Landor, "which necessarily must occur to minds of the like magnitude and materials, aspect and temperature. When two nations are in the same phasis, they will excite the same humors, and produce the same coincidences and combinations." Coleridge's sublime Hymn before Sunrise in the Vale of Chamouni has been pronounced an audacious plagiarism from a German poetess; but Coleridge, in the generous judgment of the critic, did his plundering grandly; he was like the white-headed American eagle, which swoops down with force enough to seize the whole prey from his fellow, and soar with it unmutilated in its beak. Frances Anne Kemble in Old Woman's Gossip preserves a charming instance of naive ignorance in a young guardsman, reduced by the enthusiasm of the gay society of London into going, for once, to see a play of Shakespeare's. After sitting dutifully through some scenes in silence, he turned to a fellow-guardsman, who was painfully looking and listening by his side, with the grave remark, "I say, George, doocèd odd play this; it's all full of quotations." The young military gentleman had occasionally, it seems, heard Shakespeare quoted, and remembered it. "What is a great man," asks Emerson, "but one of great affinities, who takes up into himself all arts, sciences, all knowables, as his food? Every book is a quotation; and every house is a quotation out of all forests, and mines, and stone quarries; and every man is a quotation from all his ancestors." "People are always talking," said Goethe, "about originality; but what do they mean? As soon as we are born, the world begins to work upon us, and this goes on to the end." "So far as respects my own taste," says the author of Modern Chivalry, "I read with great pleasure oftentimes a book which has not a single idea in it from beginning to end except in the quotations. The only question that is made by me, is

Guardsman and one of Shakespeare's plays.

Every man a quotation.

the quotation from a good author, or does it amuse or instruct. Nor in reading good moral observations, or anecdotes of great men, do I care whether they are in a connected series, or strung together like Swift's Tritical Dissertation on the Faculties of the Human Mind. The Apophthegms of Plutarch are somewhat in the same way. The chapters of Athenæus, and the Noctes Atticæ of Aulus Gellius, are of the same rambling sort of composition. Montaigne's Essays also; and some of the introductory chapters of Henry Fielding." A distinguished actor, playwright, and dramatist, defending himself against a charge of plagiarism, says: "On looking through the list *The great dramatic writers.* of the works of our great dramatic writers, I fail to perceive that Sheridan has acknowledged that out of his seven works five are adaptations, and the other two far from 'original.' Wycherley's four works are all 'taken from the French.' Vanbrugh and Farquhar freely altered old plays, or, like Molière, 'took their plots and characters where they could find them.' It would puzzle Messrs. Collier and Grant White to find one of Shakespeare's plays that could be certified as his own, so far as construction is concerned. With the exception of

Farquhar, who admitted that he had used Fletcher's Wild Goose Chase in the construction of his comedy, The Inconstant, I am not aware that any of our great dramatists have thought fit to announce the sources from which they drew their materials." Alfred Henry Huth, in his Life and Writings of Henry Thomas Buckle, expresses himself upon originality in literature: "Dante avows his obligations to Virgil, a poet himself greatly dependent on Homer, and who, in his turn, has inspired most of the heroic poets of the Middle Ages. Ariosto has been greatly indebted to him, to Ovid, and even to Horace. Shakespeare has no original plots. Spenser is deeply indebted to Ariosto, and we find at least one example of a very important idea common both to him and Shakespeare. Milton, too, is a boundless borrower. Each one improves a little or draws new truths from the works of his predecessors. Nor are the prose writers of fiction any more original than the poets. From the earliest times before stories were committed to writing their universal origin was in a fact, such as a love story or a fight. This was told in various forms, incidents were added, stories divided, and mixed and made new

All borrowers.

Milton a "boundless borrower."

again. Thus Spenser introduced an island full of allegorical personages into his Faëry Queen, which was after the fashion of many productions of this period; this gave birth to Fletcher's Purple Island, which produced Bernard's Isle of Man, from which, in its turn, arose Bunyan's Pilgrim's Progress. His description of Vanity Fair was probably taken from Bartholomew Fair or his own experiences, as characters are taken from life by various authors and worked up into different forms: and so, too, with feelings, that are common to the human race; for Dante and he both open with the same sort of description of tribulation and doubt. Swift, again, in his Gulliver's Travels, Fontenelle in his Plurality of Worlds, Voltaire in his Micromegas, are all indebted to Bergerac. Even Lord Macaulay's New Zealander is believed by some to have been taken from a conceit of Gibbon's; Sheridan's Mrs. Malaprop from Fielding's Mrs. Slipslop; Dickens owes his style and many of his incidents, such as the Duel and Samuel Weller's offer of money to Pickwick, to Smollett, and Weller's story of the muffins in all probability to Beauclerk's account to Johnson of the tragical end of Mr. Fitzherbert. Indeed, a

After the fashion.

Macaulay's New Zealander again.

man who was really original in everything would be a very prodigy, as great a prodigy as a new animal not derived from some similar ancestor. There is no single work whose dependence may not be traced upward from suggester to suggester until its origin is lost in antiquity, and it only remains for us to infer from analogous cases that it originated in some fact." It is said that Dr. Johnson at one time projected a work to show how small a quantity of real fiction there is in the world; and that the same images, with very little variation, have served all the authors who have ever written. Yet, as Coleridge has remarked, plagiarists are always suspicious of being stolen from, as pickpockets are observed commonly to walk with their hands in their breeches pockets. As well said, a writer soon finds himself in a strait. If he read much, and have a poor verbal memory, the bare seed of a thought may drop down into his life while the husk is forgotten; by and by that idea comes bubbling up to the surface of his mind; he snatches the prismatic thing as his own, and if he do not bethink himself quickly, he is indicted as a plagiarist. If he read little, but is given to his own explorations,

An original man a prodigy.

The writer in a strait.

he is pretty sure to make the same discoveries that others have made before him. *Holmes' conclusion.* Honest thinkers, Holmes says, are always stealing unconsciously from each other. Our minds are full of waifs and estrays which we think are our own. Innocent plagiarism turns up everywhere. Our best musical critic tells us that a few notes of the air of Shoo Fly are borrowed from a movement in one of the magnificent harmonies of Beethoven.

One Quality of the Great. The greatest edifice that man has ever raised was, to Madame de Staël, the most sublime monument in Rome, and the more so that it at first baffles and disappoints the mind. "One reaches the sublime only by degrees. Infinite distances separate it from that which is only beautiful. St. *St Peter's.* Peter's is a work of man which produces on the mind the effect of a marvel of nature. In it the genius of man is glorified by the magnificence of nature." I have never in my life, said Madame de Genlis, seen but two things which surpassed all that my imagination could picture to me beforehand; these are the Ocean and St. Peter's at Rome. "I have been four or five times at St. Peter's," says Hawthorne, "and always with pleasure, because there is such a delightful, summer-like warmth the moment we pass beneath the heavy padded leather curtains that protect the entrances. It is almost impossible not to believe that this genial temperature is the result of furnace-heat, but, really, it is the warmth of last summer, which will be included within these massive walls, and in that vast immensity of space, till, six months hence, this winter's chill will just have made its way thither. It would be an excellent place for a valetudinarian to lodge during the winter in St. Peter's, perhaps establishing his household in one of the papal tombs." "When the visitor," says Hillard, "has passed into the interior of St. Peter's, and so far recovered from the first rush of tumultuous sensations which crowd upon him as to be able to look about him, he will be struck with, and, if not forewarned, disappointed at, the apparent want of magnitude." But he will find that the windows of the church are never opened, it is so immense as well as so complete; that it has its own atmosphere, and needs no supply from the world without; that the most zealous professor of ventilation would admit that there was

Its genial temperature.

An atmosphere of its own.

no work for him to do here. "When we dream of the climate of heaven, we make it warmth without heat, and coolness without cold, like that of St. Peter's." "To see the Pope," exclaimed Northcote, "give the benediction at St. Peter's! raising himself up and spreading out his hands in the form of a cross, with an energy and dignity as if he was giving a blessing to the whole world!" Such a church as St. Mark's, a visitor has remarked, cannot be conquered without time. It must be visited again and again, and slowly and patiently studied. To dispatch such an edifice in an hour or two is like trying to read through Gibbon at a sitting. Long before the task is completed, the eye refuses to look, and the wearied brain to receive impressions, and we find that in attempting to grasp everything we retain nothing. The great wall of China, extending for twelve hundred English miles along what was once the whole northern frontier of the Chinese empire, — from twenty to twenty-five feet high, — wide enough for six horses to run abreast, and furnished with a suitable number of gates and bastions, contains, it has been carefully estimated, more material than all the buildings of the British empire put together. The Amazon, the mightiest river in the world, rises amid the loftiest volcanoes on the globe, and flows through a forest unparalleled in extent. We have no proper conception, says Orton, of the vast dimensions of the thousand-armed river till we sail for weeks over its broad bosom, beholding it sweeping disdainfully by the great Madeira as if its contribution was of no account, discharging into the sea one hundred thousand cubic feet of water per second more than our Mississippi, rolling its turbid waves thousands of miles exactly as it pleases, — plowing a new channel every year, with tributaries twenty miles wide, and an island in its mouth twice the size of Massachusetts. In the oceanic river, observes a Cambridge professor, the tidal action has an annual instead of a daily ebb and flow; it obeys a larger orb, and is ruled by the sun and not by the moon. Wallace says that when, for the first time, the traveler wanders in the primeval forests of the tropics, he can scarcely fail to experience sensations of awe, akin to those excited by the trackless ocean or the Alpine snowfields. There is a vastness, a solemnity, a gloom, a sense of solitude and of human insignificance

The mighty Amazon.

Primeval forests of the tropics.

which for a time overwhelms him. It has been remarked by every one who has seen the pyramids that the sense of sight is deceived in the attempt to appreciate their distance and magnitude. Though removed several leagues from the spectator, they appear to be close at hand; and it is not until he has traveled some miles in a direct line toward them that he becomes sensible of their vast bulk and also of the pure atmosphere through which they are viewed. One of the French philosophers who accompanied Napoleon to Egypt tells us that when he first visited the great pyramid he was surprised to see it so diminutive. It stood alone in a boundless plain. There was nothing near it from which to calculate its magnitude. But when the camp was pitched beside it, and the tents appeared like insignificant specks around its base, he then perceived the immensity of this mightiest work of man. It has been regarded a weakness of practical natures to laugh with Pliny at the pyramids, as mere monuments of human vanity. We forget the human weakness of personal commemoration when we remember that the pyramids are material records of a belief in immortality, the oldest and the most enduring.

The pyramids.

Records of a belief in immortality.

It is easy to preach, but not so easy to practice. We know so much better than we do. It has been said that when Charles Lamb called Coleridge "an archangel — a little damaged," he painted the contrast between human ideals and human experience. The poet Gray speaks of the Greek sophist that got immortal honor by discoursing so feelingly on the miseries of our condition, that fifty of his audience went home and hanged themselves, — the orator (the poet supposes) living many years after in very good plight. "The Greeks," says About, "who are the least scrupulous as to honesty, observe very strictly the precepts of the Church, and blindly obey the priests. When a mother sells her daughter to a rich person, she always stipulates that so much shall be given for the daughter, so much for the parents, and so much for the Church. I have had the honor," he says, "of dining with an assassin, and the misfortune of shocking him. We were at Ægina, and we were eating a lamb à la Pilikar, in the open air, and in the middle of Lent. A Greek, whom we did not know, came and sat down by us, ate our bread and our figs, drank our wine, and withdrew, much shocked at our conduct, after

Precept and Practice.

Ideals and experience.

Dining with an assassin.

he was filled. I learned next day that this sulky guest had the death of a man upon his conscience, and that justice was looking for him prudently, in such a way as never to find him. He thought himself, however, a better Christian than we." Sir James Mackintosh spent ten years in India, and the account he gives of the Hindoo character is very curious. He says in refinement of manners, cultivation, and politeness, they are equal to Europeans; they talk of truth, honor, and moral obligation as if they felt it, but that in fact they neither act upon their principles themselves nor expect you to act upon them. Sir James knew a Hindoo rajah, a man of great acquirements and of the most polished manners, who, when he was disappointed in the collection of his taxes of the sum he expected, ordered a pound of eyes to be brought him of those who had refused to pay the taxes. "I never can make out how it is," says Ruskin, "that a knight-errant does not expect to be paid for his trouble, but a peddler-errant always does; — that people are willing to take hard knocks for nothing, but never to sell ribbons cheap; — that they are ready to go on fervent crusades to recover the tomb of

A better Christian.

A pound of eyes.

a buried God, never on any travel to fulfill the orders of a living God; — that they will go anywhere barefoot to preach their faith, but must be well bribed to practice it; and are perfectly ready to give the gospel gratis, but never the loaves and fishes." It has been remarked that in the propagation of a new religion, or in a new tenet of a particular faith, what is moderate will be less likely to prevail in the opinions of men. The absurd is always the most popular, and this upon the principle that artificial tastes are stronger than the natural; and what produces the greatest excitement is most pleasing to the mind. Hence it is that mere morality and the dictates of nature and truth in the conduct of men are undervalued in comparison of the dogmata of fanatical faiths. Unintelligible reveries are better relished in the pulpit than just reasoning on the principles of right and wrong in the actions of men; and incomprehensible theological disquisitions are put into the hands of young people, as more substantial food for the mind than precepts of moral truth, which every step in life will bring into practice, and explain. Hume says in one of his essays that "if we should suppose, what never happens,

The absurd the most popular.

Incomprehensible theological disquisitions.

that a popular religion were found in which it was expressly declared that nothing but morality could gain the divine favor; if an order of priests were instituted to inculcate this opinion, in daily sermons, and with all the arts of persuasion; yet so inveterate are the people's prejudices, that, for want of some other superstition, they would make the very attendance on these sermons the essentials of religion, rather than place them in virtue and good morals."

The people's prejudices.

"No man," says Dr. Johnson, "practices as well as he preaches. I have," he said, "all my life long, been lying till noon; yet I tell all young men, and tell them with great sincerity, that nobody who does not rise early will ever do any good. Only consider! You read a book; you are convinced by it; you do not know the author. Suppose you afterwards know him, and find that he does not practice what he teaches; are you to give up your former convictions?" Foster, in a note to one of his essays, refers to a Spanish story of a village where the devil, having made the people excessively wicked, was punished by being compelled to assume the appearance and habit of a friar, and to preach so eloquently, in spite of his internal repug-

The devil compelled to turn preacher.

nance and rage, that the inhabitants were completely reformed. When Dr. Johnson said of old Lord Townshend, "though a Whig, he had humanity," he meant to say that his lordship's actions were better than his notions. A profoundly Christian man, and very practical in his Christianity, once said to me of a certain set of prominent Americans, "Though infidels, there is this to say in their favor, — they are all philanthropists." That journey of life's conquest, in which hills over hills, and Alps on Alps arose, and sank, — do you think you can make another trace it painlessly by talking? asks Ruskin. Why, you cannot even carry us up an Alp, by talking. You can guide us up to it, step by step, no otherwise — even so, best silently. It is the expressed opinion of Taine that in the matter of morals, words amount to nothing; in themselves, they are only so many more or less disagreeable sounds. It is the education precedent which gives them force and meaning. If this have lodged two or three sensible ideas in the boy's head, talk rationally to him; if not, as well attempt to strike sparks from a log of wood. You must address yourself to feelings which already exist, and no fine

Actions better than notions.

Words amount to nothing.

phrases can call them into life in a quarter of an hour. Dr. Thomson said of Godwin (who, in the full tide of his theory of perfectibility, declared he "could educate tigers"), "I should like to see him in a cage with two of his pupils."

Godwin's theory of perfectibility.

To speak short, think long, is the advice of wisdom to speakers and writers. Can it be that Paley meant to enforce the admonition, when in one of his College Lectures he urged the clergy, if their situation required a sermon every Sunday, to "make one and steal five"? Though, so far as the English Church is concerned, a witty traveler has described the standard of the sermons in the Establishment to be, "twenty minutes in length and no depth at all."

LONG SERMONS.

Of all preachers, according to Joceline, St. Patrick was the most tremendous. He went through the four Gospels in one exposition to the Irish at a place called Finnablair, and he was three days and nights about it, without intermission, to the great delight of the hearers, who thought that only one day had passed. St. Bridget was present, and she took a comfortable nap, and had a vision.

St. Patrick's preaching.

It was wisely observed by Swift that every man desireth to live long, but nobody would be old. In one of Lucian's Dialogues of the Dead is reported a conversation between an old man and Diogenes. The philosopher, seeing all but infants in tears, asks, in extreme surprise, whether life can exercise some spell or charm over mankind, so as to induce even the aged to deplore its loss. "What can be the cause of your sorrow?" says he to the old man. "You were, perhaps, once a sovereign?" "No." "At least a satrap?" "No." "A man of great wealth, then?" "No; nothing of the kind; only a beggar of fourscore and ten years, scarcely supporting life with a rod and line, childless, lame, and blind." "And having been such, you yet desire to live as such again?" "Yea, verily," replies the beggar, "for life is sweet, and death is dire and detestable." Lucian also reports an interview between Cerberus and Menippus as to Socrates, in the same dark region. "Cerberus, I beseech you, by Styx, to inform me how Socrates behaved when he came down amongst you: I suppose, being a god, you can talk as well as bark, when you have a mind to it." "At first, Menippus," Cer-

Old Age.

An old man and Diogenes.

Socrates.

berus replied, "and whilst he was at a good distance, the philosopher never looked back, but advanced boldly forwards, seeming not to fear death in the least, and as if he meant to show his bravery to those who stood afar off from the centre of Tartarus; but when he came into the cave, and found it all dark and dismal, and, to hasten him a little, I bit him by his poisoned foot, he cried like a child, began to lament his children, and writhed about."

Seemed not at first to fear death.

It was Sir William Temple's opinion that life is like wine; who would drink it pure must not draw it to the dregs. "I abhor," said Emerson to Carlyle, "the inroads which time makes on me and my friends. To live too long is the capital misfortune." In his closing years, life appeared to Humboldt increasingly in the light of Dante's celebrated simile, as a race to death, an expression he loved to quote. At eighty-eight he wrote to one of his friends: "Pray avoid living to so unusual an age."

A saying of Solon.

Solon used to say to his friends that a man of sixty ought never to fear death nor to complain of the evils of life. He might have said, further, that a man at that time of life has already lived nearly twice his right, according to the average, and that for so many years he has lived upon other people's time.

"I am," said Sydney Smith, "going slowly down the hill of life. One evil in old age is, that as your time is come, you think every little illness is the beginning of the end. When a man expects to be arrested, every knock at the door is an alarm. We are, at the close of life, only hurried away from stomach-aches, pains in the joints, from sleepless nights and unamusing days, from weakness, ugliness, and nervous tremors." "I suspect," he said, at another time, "the fifth act of life should be in great cities; it is there, in the long death of old age, that a man most forgets himself and his infirmities; receives the greatest consolation from the attentions of friends, and the greatest diversion from external circumstances." *One evil in old age.*

"Youth," thought Souvestre, "is a forced apprenticeship, in which one's time, will, intelligence, everything, is the property of one's master. Our feet carry us well, but stir only at the word of command. Manhood imposes on us fresh duties at every instant; middle life increases the burden of our responsibilities; old age alone is really free. The world of which *Old age alone is really free.*

we were slaves signs then, at length, our order of release. Ours are henceforth the long nights of repose, the walks without any defined object, the uninterrupted chit-chats, the whimsical readings, the hours spent at one's ease; no longer have we at our doors the six week days crying out to us like Bluebeard in the popular tale, 'Will you come down there from above?'"

The hours spent at one's ease.

"The time that we count by the year has gone, and the time that we must count by the day comes in its stead. The less one's income, the more important to use it well. I have (says Diderot) perhaps half a score of years at the bottom of my wallet. In these ten years, fluxions, rheumatisms, and the other members of that troublesome family will take two or three of them; let us try to economize the seven that are left, for the repose and the small happiness that a man may promise himself on the wrong side of sixty."

Charlotte Brontë thought that at best life is so constructed that the event does not, cannot, will not, match the experience.

Events and experiences.

When Hogarth's life was nearly done he made a picture showing the end of all earthly things. On the canvas was a shattered bottle, a cracked bell, an unstrung bow, the sign-post of a tavern called The World's End falling down, a shipwreck, the horses of Phœbus lying dead in the clouds, the moon in her last quarter, the world on fire. "One more thing," said Hogarth, "and I have done." Then he added to this picture a painter's palette broken. It was the last work of art he ever executed. *Hogarth's last picture.*

Montaigne said, "God is favorable to those whom he makes to die by degrees; 't is the only benefit of old age; the last death will be so much the less full and painful; it will kill but a half or quarter of a man." "We do not die wholly at our deaths," said Hazlitt; "we have mouldered away gradually long before. Faculty after faculty, interest after interest, attachment after attachment disappear: we are torn from ourselves while living, year after year sees us no longer the same, and death only consigns the last fragment of what we were to the grave." Dr. Oliver Wendell Holmes revisited England when he was seventy-five years old. "One incident of our excursion to Stonehenge," he says, "had a significance to me which renders it memorable in my personal experience. As we drove over the barren plain, one of the *A touching incident of Holmes.*

party suddenly exclaimed, 'Look! Look! See the lark rising!' I looked up with the rest. There was the bright blue sky, but not a speck upon it which my eyes could distinguish. Again, one called out, 'Hark! Hark! Hear him singing!' I listened, but not a sound reached my ear. Was it strange that I felt a momentary pang? Those that look out of the windows are darkened, and all the daughters of music are brought low. Was I never again to see or hear the soaring songster at Heaven's Gate?" Donald MacLeod describes the visit of Walter Scott to London, four years before his death. The decay of his powers was already very apparent. He spent six weeks with the Lockharts and with his son Charles. Here were old friends yet to welcome him, and quiet dinners with the king and others. He goes about, one day to hear Coleridge discourse on the Samothracian Mysteries, another day to sit to the artist Northcote: again to exchange a lock of his white hair with a pretty girl for a kiss, and once to hear a lady sing one of his own songs from the Pirate:—

Scott, four years before his death.

"Farewell, farewell, the voice you hear
   Has left its last soft tones with you,
Its next must join the seaward cheer,
   And shout amid the shouting crew."

He liked the music, and whispered to Lockhart, "Capital words: whose are they? Byron's, I suppose, but I don't remember them." When told that they were his own, he seemed pleased for an instant, but the pleasure vanished, and he said, "You have distressed me. If memory goes, all is gone with me, for that was always my strong point." Oblivion was scattering her poppy. *Memory gone.*

The wonder is that we should care so much to remain here — those of us that have felt successively the touches of decay. Dim eyes, dull ears, lost teeth, flaccid muscles, trembling nerves, uncertain locomotion, impaired memory, remind us of what we were, and warn us of what we will be if we linger. Fading, failing, is announced in every function and faculty. We have had our little day. We did our poor best in the fight that is over. We have known the inspiration of effort and the delights of achievement. We have received about all we deserved. Poor or rich, we have had our joys and our anxieties. Our sons are fairly on the way. We have built houses for them, to be superseded or remodeled. We are at the tail of the procession. It is easy to see that society has arranged to *Fading, failing.*

do without us. Our notions are obsolete or superannuated. They call us names when we express them. We hang our faces on the wall, to be turned to it in time, and forgotten. Our reason is called obstinacy. *In the way of progress.* We are in the way of progress, and a hindrance to growth. Our little savings are anticipated capital. Life insurance has made our deaths interesting. We cling to old clothes, old customs, old associations, and acquired habits, and are laughed at by those who will do the same. Our minds have been traveled over till those who are familiar with us take for granted they know them better than we know them ourselves. When we open our mouths they assume to know precisely what we mean to say. The point of our talk is anticipated and made easy. Circumspection is imbecility, experience distrust. Our signs of things are invisibilities, which are revealed only to ourselves by introspection and the gravest reflection. *Why should we want to stay?* Why should we want to stay, where we are not wanted, and can do little good, — where impulse and inexperience are to govern? Experience is for philosophers, and philosophy is not less hateful than moderation. To our tombs we should go as consciously and uncomplainingly as we go to our beds.

"The old," says Goethe, "lose one of the greatest privileges of man, they are no longer judged by their contemporaries." Northcote said, "What takes off the edge and stimulus of exertion in old age, is: those who were our competitors in early life, whom we wished to excel or whose good opinion we were most anxious about, are gone, and have left us in a manner by ourselves, in a sort of new world, where we know and are as little known as on entering a strange country. Our ambition is cold with the ashes of those whom we feared or loved." "As for envy," said Plutarch, "which is the greatest evil attending the management of public affairs, it least attacks old age. For dogs indeed, as Heraclitus has it, bark at a stranger whom they do not know; and envy opposes him who is a beginner on the very steps of the tribune, hindering his access, but she meekly bears an accustomed and familiar glory, and not churlishly or with difficulty. Wherefore some resemble envy to smoke; for it arises thick at first, when the fire begins to burn; but when the flame grows clear, it vanishes away."

Stimulus of exertion taken off.

Envy reconciled.

It is a maxim of La Rochefoucauld's that "Old men delight in giving good advice, as a consolation for the fact that they can no longer set bad examples." Which reminds one of a passage in quaint old Roger Ascham's Schoolmaster: "It is a notable tale that old Sir Roger Chamloe, sometime chief justice, would tell of himself. When he was Ancient in inn of court, certain young gentlemen were brought before him to be corrected for certain misorders; and one of the lustiest said: 'Sir, we be young gentlemen; and wise men before we have proved all fashions, and yet those have done well.' This they said because it was well known Sir Roger had been a good fellow in his youth. But he answered them very wisely. 'Indeed,' saith he, 'in youth I was as you are now; and I had twelve fellows like unto myself, but not one of them came to a good end. And therefore, follow not my example in youth, but follow my counsel in age, if ever ye think to come to this place, or to these years, that I am come unto; less you meet either with poverty or Tyburn in the way.'"

Cato the Elder begged of old men not to add the disgrace of wickedness to old

A quaint passage.

Counsel in age.

age, which was accompanied by many other evils. "Certainly Mr. Shelley is right in his notions about old age," thought De Quincey; "unless powerfully counteracted by all sorts of opposite agencies, it is a miserable corrupter and blighter to the genial charities of the human heart." *An observation of De Quincey's.*

"The unthinking think," says a wise contemporary, "that death is an evil. It may be to the individual. It is fortunate that he has not the choice. As evil is requisite to good, so death is requisite to life. If men did not die, men could not be born. Without the passing away and the ever renewal of life, the world would be like a living thing chained to a corpse."

"Death is in one thing very good," said La Bruyère: "it puts an end to old age." Goethe, in the second part of Faust, represents his hero, in blind old age, cultivating the barren sea sand. Swift said, "It is impossible that anything so natural, so necessary, and so universal as death should ever have been designed by Providence as an evil to mankind." *A saying of Swift's.*

The famous French chemist, Chevreul, now over one hundred years old, told a friend "the secret of long living." I have never been, he said, "a pessimist, and I have continually kept myself from being too much of an optimist. Let us not trouble ourselves about to-morrow. Let us enjoy the present." Bonstetten, a lifelong friend of Madame de Staël, and who died at ninety, wrote: "To resist with success the frigidity of old age, one must combine the body, the mind, and the heart; to keep these in parallel vigor, one must exercise, study, and love."

Enjoy the present.

"It would," says Addison, in The Tatler, "be a good appendix to the Art of Living and Dying, if any one would write the Art of Growing Old, and teach men to resign their pretensions to the pleasures and gallantries of youth, in proportion to the alteration they find in themselves by the approach of age and infirmities. The infirmities of this stage of life would be much fewer, if we did not affect those which attend the more vigorous and active part of our days; but, instead of studying to be wiser, or being contented with our present follies, the ambition of many of us is also to be the same sort of fools we formerly have been." A short time before Colley Cibber's death, Horace Walpole hailed him, on his birthday, with a good morning, and "I am glad, sir, to see you

A foolish ambition.

looking so well." "Egad, sir," replied the old gentleman — all diamonded and powdered, and dandified — "at eighty-four, it's well for a man that he can look at all." *Colley Cibber at eighty-four.*

"There are lives," says Philip Gilbert Hamerton, "such as that of Major Pendennis, which only diminish in value as they advance — when the man of fashion is no longer fashionable, and the sportsman can no longer stride over the ploughed fields. The old age of the Pendennises is assuredly not to be envied; but how rich is the age of the Humboldts! I compare the life of the intellectual to a long wedge of gold — the thin edge of it begins at birth, and the depth and value of it go on indefinitely increasing till at last comes Death, who stops the auriferous processes." *The Pendennises and the Humboldts.*

The only way, Steele thought, of avoiding a trifling and frivolous old age is to lay up in our way to it such stores of knowledge and observation as may make us useful and agreeable in our declining years. The mind of man in a long life will become a magazine of wisdom or folly, and will consequently discharge itself in something impertinent or improving. For which reason, as there is nothing more ridiculous than an old trifling story-teller, so there is *The mind a magazine of wisdom or folly.*

nothing more venerable than one who has turned his experience to the entertainment and advantage of mankind. In short, we, who are in the last stage of life, and are apt to indulge ourselves in talk, ought to consider if what we speak be worth being heard, and endeavor to make our discourse like that of Nestor, which Homer compares to the flowing of honey for its sweetness.

Worth considering.

Mrs. Piozzi, when she was past eighty, wrote affectionate love letters and gave presents to a handsome actor named Conway, with whom she was passionately in love.

Madame de Pompadour, hearing that Crébillon was very poor in his old age, induced the king to allow him a pension of an hundred louis. Crébillon hastened to thank his benefactress. She was confined to bed with a slight indisposition, when he was announced; she desired him to be admitted. Affected by the sight of this fine old man, she gave him a very gracious reception. He was affected by it, and was leaning on the bed to kiss her hand, when the king came in. "Ah, madame," cried Crébillon, "the king has surprised us; I am undone."

Crébillon.

Surprised by the king.

"I am grown older by many years," says Montaigne, "since my first publication;

but I very much doubt whether I am grown an inch the wiser. I now, and I anon, are two several persons ; but whether the better now, or anon, I am not able to determine. It were a fine thing to be old, if we only traveled toward improvement; but 'tis a drunken, stumbling, reeling, ill-favored motion, like that of reeds, which the air casually waves to and fro at pleasure. Antiochus, in his youth, vigorously wrote in favor of the Academy ; and in his old age he wrote against it. Would not which of these two soever I should follow be still Antiochus ?"

Two several persons.

"I have lived," says Thoreau, "some thirty years on this planet, and I have yet to hear the first syllable of valuable or even earnest advice from my seniors. They have told me nothing, and probably cannot tell me anything, to the purpose. Here is life, an experiment to a great extent untried by me ; but it does not avail me that they have tried it. If I have any experience which I think valuable, I am sure to reflect that this my Mentors said nothing about."

Life an experiment.

"People always fancy," said Goethe, laughing, "that we must become old to become wise ; but, in truth, as years advance, it is hard to keep ourselves as wise as we were. Man becomes, indeed, in the different stages of his life, a different being; but he cannot say that he is a better one, and, in certain matters, he is as likely to be right in his twentieth, as in his sixtieth year. We see the world one way from a plain, another way from the heights of a promontory, another from the glacial fields of the primary mountains. We see, from one of these points, a larger piece of the world than from the other, but that is all, and we cannot say that we see more truly from any one than from the rest." "Age ought to make us tolerant," he said on another occasion; "I never see a fault which I did not myself commit."

In different stages a different being.

It is stated that when Harvey announced to the world his great discovery of the circulation of the blood, among the physicians who received it there was not one above the age of forty.

Transplanting old people has been likened to transplanting old trees; a twelvemonth usually sees them wither and die away. Grattan said of Flood, who was brought late into Parliament, as Cobbett and Jeffrey, that "the oak of the forest was too old to be transplanted at sixty."

Transplanting old people.

Lady Mary Wortley Montagu wrote to her husband, "'T is a maxim with me to be young as long as one can: there is nothing can pay one for that invaluable ignorance which is the companion of youth: those sanguine groundless hopes, and that lively vanity, which make up the happiness of life. To my extreme mortification, I grow wiser every day." *A good maxim.*

Content is not. Youth would hasten the hours, age arrest them altogether. Time! "Nothing is so short, when we wish to complete a work; nothing can creep slower when we are expecting, or fly more rapidly when we are enjoying pleasure; nothing is more divisible, or can be more extensive, more neglected, or more regretted when lost; nothing can be done without it: Time swallows all that is unworthy to reach posterity, and immortalizes all that is great and wise."

"Eternity! What is that?" was asked at the Deaf and Dumb Institution at Paris, and the beautiful and striking answer was given by one of the pupils, "The lifetime of the Almighty." *Eternity.*

Cicero puts these words into the mouth of his hero, in his Dialogue on Old Age: "The day of my death it will not be easy

No desire to be "recast."

to retain me here below. I do not desire to be 'recast,' like Pelias; if some god thought of conferring on me a favor by proposing to me to recommence my journey from infancy, and to crawl about a second time in swaddling-clothes, I should refuse unhesitatingly. The race being run, I have no desire to be recalled from the goal to the starting-point. Not that I affect to depreciate life, as certain philosophers have often done; I do not repent having lived, because I think I have lived so as not to have been born in vain; but I shall quit existence as an inn, and not as a dwelling-place. Nature has given man the material world that he may stay there awhile; she does not condemn him to remain forever. O happy day! when I shall escape from the crowd and from the mire, to rejoin the celestial assembly, the divine senate of souls."

The divine senate of souls.

There are lives, it has been said, that are so rounded and crowned by their completed deeds of love, that death seems to have appeared in the fullness of their prime only to consecrate them forever; others stand apart from human ties in a solitude which makes time seem of little consequence, and the grave a not unfamiliar country. Solitude is often less solitary than society — where solitude is calm and clear; solitude only brings home to one one's own isolation. At all events, the evidence of a hundred death-beds, of the utmost diversity, entirely goes to prove, that among sincere and high-minded men and women, death appears to be rather a process of coming to one's self, of entering into a certain calm and self-possession, than one of pain, of alarm, or even of surprise. *Evidence of death-beds.*

A short time before Maria Theresa, queen of Hungary and Bohemia, breathed her last, having apparently fallen into a sort of insensibility, and her eyes being closed, one of the ladies near her person, in reply to an inquiry respecting the state of the empress, answered that her majesty seemed to be asleep. "No," replied she; "I could sleep if I would indulge repose; but I am sensible of the near approach of death, and I will not allow myself to be surprised by him in my sleep. I wish to meet my dissolution awake." *Wished to meet her dissolution awake.*

On an old parchment, in Arabic, is inscribed, "I came to the place of my birth, and cried, 'The friends of my youth, where are they?' and Echo answered, 'Where are they?'" "I am grown so old," said Dr. Franklin, at eighty-two, "as to have buried most of the friends of my youth; and I now often hear persons, whom I knew when children, called old Mr. Such-a-one, to distinguish them from their sons, now men grown and in business; so that, by living twelve years beyond David's period, I seem to have intruded myself into the company of posterity, when I ought to have been abed and asleep. . . . I look upon death to be as necessary to our constitutions as sleep. We shall rise refreshed in the morning." "When I look around me," said Goethe, "and see how few of the companions of earlier years are left to me, I think of a summer residence at a bathing-place. When you arrive, you first become acquainted with those who have already been there some weeks, and who leave you in a few days. This separation is painful. Then you turn to the second generation, with which you live a good while, and become really intimate. But this goes also, and leaves us lonely with the third, which comes just as we are going away, and with which we have properly nothing to do." Charles Lamb, in a letter to one of his distant correspondents, im-

Margin notes:
Life at eighty-two.
Life like a summer residence at a bathing-place.

plores him to "come back." "Come back," he says, "before I am grown into a very old man, so as you shall hardly know me. Come before Bridget walks on crutches. Girls whom you left children have become sage matrons while you are tarrying there. The blooming Miss W——r (you remember Sally W——) called upon us yesterday, an aged crone. Folks, whom you knew, die off every year. Formerly, I thought that death was wearing out, — I stood ramparted about with so many healthy friends. The departure of J. W., two springs back, corrected my delusion. Since then the old divorcer has been busy. If you do not make haste to return there will be little left to greet you, of me, or mine." John Kenyon, writing a note of sympathy to Crabb Robinson, on occasion of the death of his grand-nephew, said, "Only live on, and this once smiling world is changed into a huge cemetery, in which we ourselves hardly care to linger." There is a Turkish tale to the effect that when Solomon was ruling on earth, the angel Gabriel was sent to him one day with a goblet filled with the water of life, and bearing from on high the message that, if he chose, he might drink of the water and

Girls become sage matrons.

A Turkish tale.

become immortal. Calling together all his wisest counselors, he asked their advice. They, with one consent, advised him to drink and live forever. Then he summoned the birds of the air and the beasts of the field, and all of them gave the same advice, with one solitary exception. *The hedgehog's advice to Solomon.* This was the hedgehog. Approaching the throne, and bending its brow to the ground, thus did it speak: "If this water may be shared by thee with thy kith and kin, then drink and enjoy the bliss of living. But if it is intended for thee alone, then do not drink. For sad would it be for thee to live on, but to see thy kinsmen and friends one after the other disappear." "True are thy words, O hedgehog!" replied Solomon. "To me alone has the water of life been sent. As thou hast counseled so will I decide." And the water of life did he not drink.

Protesilaus and Pluto. You remember the touching dialogue in Lucian, between Protesilaus and Pluto: "O Pluto! our great lord and master, the Jupiter of these regions of the dead, and thou, daughter of Ceres, despise not a lover's prayer?" "What would you ask of us, friend, and who are you?" said Pluto. "I am Protesilaus, the Phylacian, son of

Iphiclus, an ally of the Grecians, and was the first man slain at Troy: my desire is, that I may return back, and live a little longer." "That is a desire, Protesilaus, which all the dead have; but which was never granted to any." "It is not," said Protesilaus, "for the sake of living, but on account of my wife, whom I had just married, and left in her bridal-bed, when I set out on my voyage, and, unfortunately, the moment I landed, was slain by Hector: the love of her makes me very unhappy; all I wish for is but to see her for a short time, and return to you again." "Have not you drank the waters of Lethe?" asked Pluto. "I have," answered Protesilaus, "but to no purpose; this thought is still afflicting."

Desired to return back.

The waters of Lethe insufficient.

Johnson's tender affection for his departed wife, of which there are many evidences in his Prayers and Meditations, appears very feelingly in this passage from his diary kept while he was in Paris: "The sight of palaces and other great buildings leaves no very distinct images, unless to those who talk of them. As I entered the Palais Bourbon, my wife was in my mind; she would have been pleased. Having now nobody to please, I am little pleased." The old gentleman in Gil Blas, it is observed, who complained that the peaches were not as fine as they appeared to be when he was young, had more reason than appears on the face of it. He missed not only his former palate, but the places he ate them in, and those who ate them with him. When Wilkie was in the Escurial, looking at Titian's famous picture of the Last Supper, in the refectory there, an old man said to him, "I have sat daily in sight of that picture for more than threescore years, during that time my companions have dropped off, one after another, all who were my seniors, all who were my contemporaries, and many, or most of those who were younger than myself; more than one generation has passed away, and these the figures in the picture have remained unchanged. I look at them till I sometimes think that they are the realities, and we but the shadows."

Titian's famous picture.

"At the age of seventy-five," said Goethe, "one must of course think frequently of death. But this thought never gives me the least uneasiness, I am so fully convinced that the soul is indestructible, and that its activity will continue through eternity. It is like the sun, which seems to our earthly eyes to set in night,

The soul indestructible.

but is in reality gone to diffuse its light elsewhere."

> "The tomb is not an endless night;
> It is a thoroughfare — a way
> That closes in a soft twilight
> And opens in eternal day."

While waiting at the station at Uttoxeter, before his departure, Hawthorne asked a boy who stood near him — an intelligent and gentlemanly lad, twelve or thirteen years old, whom he took to be a clergyman's son — if he had ever heard the story of Dr. Johnson, how he stood an hour doing penance near that church, the spire of which rose before them. The boy stared and answered, "No!" "Were you born at Uttoxeter?" "Yes." He was asked if no circumstance such as had been mentioned was known or talked about among the inhabitants. "No," said the boy; "not that I ever heard of." "Just think," reflects the great novelist, "of the absurd little town, knowing nothing of the only memorable incident which ever happened within its boundaries since the old Britons built it, this sad and lovely story, which consecrates the spot (for I found it holy to my contemplation, again, as soon

Oblivion.

The absurd little town.

as it lay before me) in the heart of a stranger from three thousand miles over the sea!" Some years ago, a writer in Temple Bar, when in Bath, being anxious to amuse himself with verifying all the places and streets, etc., mentioned in Persuasion and Northanger Abbey, he turned into a library close to Milsom Street, and asked for the volume; he was told not only that they had not got it, but had never even heard of Jane Austen! And what was still worse, and hurt his feelings more, was that when he sought the inn which her genius had made so memorable, though he found it, lo and behold! it was no longer the White Hart, it had sunk into the Queen, or the Royal Hotel, or something equally commonplace. When Swift was desired by Lord Oxford to introduce Parnell to his acquaintance, he refused, upon this principle, that a man of genius was a character superior to that of a lord in a high station; he therefore obliged his lordship to walk with his treasurer's staff from room to room through his own department, inquiring which was Dr. Parnell, in order to introduce himself, and beg the honor of his acquaintance. Dr. James Alexander, describing a visit to the India

A writer's experience in Bath.

A man of genius and a lord.

House, says he inquired for Charles Lamb of the old doorkeeper, who replied he had been there since he was sixteen years old, and had never heard of any Mr. Lamb. But the doorkeeper of the British Museum knew him very well. Not long after Irving *Irving.* had attained celebrity in Great Britain by his writings, an English lady and her daughter were passing along some gallery in Italy and paused before a bust of Washington. After gazing at it for a few moments, the daughter turned to her mother with the question: "Mother, who was Washington?" "Why, my dear, don't you know?" was the astonished reply; "he wrote the Sketch Book." The health of Darwin was anything but good; and *Darwin.* an old family servant — a woman — overhearing his daughter express some anxiety about his condition, sought to reassure her by saying: "Hi believe master 'd be hall right, madam, hif 'e only 'ad something to hoccupy 'is mind; sometimes 'e stands in the conservatory from mornin' till night — just a lookin' at the flowers. Hif 'e only 'ad somethin' to do, 'e 'd be hevver so much better, hi'm sure." An ignorant old fellow who had known Hawthorne was met *Hawthorne.* by Mr. Harry Fenn in Salem, who vouchsafed to the artist the information that Hawthorne "writ a lot o' letters — I heern he wrote a scarlet letter or two, whatever that is." The great-grandniece of Mrs. Barbauld gives in her recently published Memories many interesting anecdotes of the writers of the last generation. Concerning Samuel Rogers, whose generosity and whose polished manners she praises, she says: "Going one night to the gallery of the opera, which he thought the best place for hearing, he noticed a respectable-looking elderly man gazing at him very intently for some time. At last between the acts he left his seat, and placing himself in front of Mr. Rogers, said in a solemn tone, 'Pray, sir, is your name Samuel Rogers?' Mr. Rogers, who always cherished the hope that his works were popular with the lower classes, replied most graciously that it was. 'Then, sir,' said the man, 'I should be glad to know, if you please, why you have changed your poulterer?'"

<small>Samuel Rogers.</small>

<small>Subsisting by Authorship.</small> Literature has been pronounced a good staff but a bad crutch, — fascinating, cheering, and enlivening, tending to promote life, health, and an equable mind in those

who pursue it for pleasure; but woe to those who are dependent upon their brains for daily bread, — thrice woe, if others are dependent upon them. Coleridge advised, never pursue literature as a trade. Hawthorne, wrote, God keep me from ever being really a writer for bread. Lamb exclaims, in a letter to Barton: "What! throw yourself on the world without any rational plan of support beyond what the chance of employment of booksellers would afford you? Throw yourself rather, my dear sir, from the steep Tarpeian rock slap-dash, headlong down upon iron spikes. I have known many authors want bread: some repining, others enjoying the sweet security of a spunging-house; all agreeing they had rather have been tailors, weavers, what not, rather than the things they were! I have known some starved — some go mad — one dear friend literally dying in a work-house. O! you know not, may you never know, the miseries of subsisting by authorship! 'T is a pretty appendage to situations like yours or mine, but a slavery worse than all slavery to be a bookseller's dependent; to drudge your brains for pots of ale and breasts of mutton; to change your free thoughts and

Literature as a trade.

A pretty appendage.

voluntary numbers for ungracious task-work! The booksellers hate us." "With the greatest possible solicitude," urged Herder, "avoid authorship. Too early or immediately employed, it makes the head waste and the heart empty; even were there no other worse consequences. A person who reads only to print, in all probability reads amiss; and he who sends away through the pen and the press every thought, the moment it occurs to him, will in a short time have sent all away, and will become a mere journeyman of the printing-office, a compositor." "Writing for the press," says John Stuart Mill, "cannot be recommended as a permanent resource to any one qualified to accomplish anything in the higher departments of literature or thought; not only on account of the uncertainty of this means of livelihood, especially if the writer has a conscience and will not consent to serve any opinions except his own, but also because the writings by which one can live are not the writings which themselves live, and are never those in which the writer does his best. Books destined to form future thinkers take too much time to write, and when written, come, in general, too slowly into

Herder's advice.

Some views of Mill's.

notice and repute to be relied on for subsistence." The mother of Agassiz — a remarkable woman — wrote to her son about the time he began to associate with Humboldt, Cuvier, and other eminent naturalists: "You know your mother's heart too well to misunderstand her thought, even should its expression be unacceptable to you. With much knowledge, acquired by assiduous industry, you are still at twenty-five years of age living on brilliant hopes, in relation, it is true, with great people, and known as having distinguished talent. Now, all this would seem to be delightful if you had an income of fifty thousand francs; but, in your position, you must absolutely have an occupation which will enable you to live, and free you from the insupportable weight of dependence on others. From this day forward, my child, you must look to this end alone if you would find it possible to pursue honorably the career you have chosen. Otherwise constant embarrassments will so limit your genius, that you will fall below your own capacity." To a young poet without fortune Voltaire wrote: "Think first to improve your circumstances. First live; then compose." In the same strain is the

The mother of Agassiz to her son.

Voltaire to a young poet.

postscript to an unpublished letter of Walter Scott's, to a reverend friend, written at the time he was hard at work on The Fair Maid of Perth: "Will you excuse my offering a piece of serious advice? Whatever pleasure you may find in literature, beware of looking to it as a profession, but seek that independence to which every one hopes to attain by studying the branch of industry which lies most within your reach. In this case you may pursue your literary amusements honorably and happily, but if ever you have to look to literature for an absolute and necessary support, you must be degraded by the necessity of writing, whether you feel inclined or not, and besides must suffer all the miseries of a precarious and dependent existence." Pitch low, adapt to the multitude, has too often been the humiliating, mercenary advice of publishers to authors. A publisher once said to Froude: "Sir, if you wish to write a book that will sell, consider the ladies' maids. Please the ladies' maids, and you please the great reading world." "The reason why these fellows hate us [meaning the publishers] I take to be," says Lamb, "that contrary to other trades, in which the master gets

Scott to a reverend friend.

A publisher to Froude.

all the credit (a jeweler or silversmith for instance), and the journeyman, who really does the fine work, is in the background; in our work the world gives all the credit to us, whom they consider as their journeymen, and therefore do they hate us, and cheat us, and oppress us, and would wring the blood of us out, to put another sixpence in their mechanic pouches." At literary dinners the health of Napoleon, who shot a publisher, will ever be a standing toast; and legends will continue to be repeated as to the existence of a precious edition of the Bible in which the misprint occurs — "publishers and sinners."

The world gives credit.

Previous to the inauguration of Humboldt's bust in Central Park, and when it was announced in the newspapers that Dr. Francis Lieber was to deliver the German speech, a friend of Lieber's was thus addressed by a car acquaintance who pointed to Lieber's name in the newspaper: "Don't you think it remarkable, sir, that a man like Dr. Lieber should publicly speak for that Helmbold and his Buchu?" — meaning the then conspicuous patent medicine vender and his commodity. "Helmbold must pay him a thundering price —

PRETENSION.

that I know." The platform orator, Mr. Parsons, had been advertised for his lecture on the great Richard Brinsley Sheridan. The president of the lecture association, before introducing the lecturer, stated to the audience that "it had been deemed advisable by the committee to change the programme for the evening; that Mr. Parsons would not lecture upon Richard Brindle Sheridan, but would, as requested, give his lecture upon The Mediterranean." The impression existed with a good many that the lecture first announced was upon Sheridan the general; they had had enough of him; they didn't want a war speech, or anything of the kind; especially they didn't want to hear recited again, for the thousandth time, Sheridan's Ride. One handsome fellow, handsomely dressed, with a handsome wife on his arm — on the way to the lecture — was heard to say, that he detested Sheridan's Ride; that he had heard it recited so often he had thought he would never hear it again; but he supposed he must be tortured by it once more. A Yorkshireman was advised to read some really good book, and Plato was mentioned as likely to suit him. Afterward he was asked, "Well, what do you think of Plato?"

In a Club Corner

"Plato? O, that Plato! I'll tell you what I think of him. He's as big a humbug as ever lived. Why, man, Emerson has said it all before him." We once heard a preacher in his sermon sweepingly condemn the writings of Alexander Pope as immoral and dangerous. At the conclusion, he read out, and effectively too — to be sung by the congregation — the beautiful hymn, "Vital spark of heavenly flame! Quit! oh quit," etc. Sitting one day in the family room reading The Spectator, a young lady of the neighborhood came in unexpectedly. To have something to say, I remarked, after greeting, that I had just picked up the old Spectator, which was always new and interesting to me. "Yes," responded the miss, lispingly; "my father subscribed for a copy when it first came out." Not knowing that the precious book was published in London a century before her father was born, and at the slow rate of a number a day. Referring casually, for purpose of illustration, to the habit of Neander, the church historian, of tearing unconsciously the feathery part of a quill to pieces while he lectured, a pretentious lady at the other end of the table, determined not to conceal her learning, inter-

Writings of Pope condemned.

Neander and the pretentious lady.

rupted, with the utmost sincerity, by exclaiming, — "That's the gentleman, I believe, who swam the Hellespont." Thirty years ago or more Thomas Starr King added to his fame as a pulpit orator by delivering throughout the country a lecture upon Socrates. A gentleman who had heard the famous lecture in the neighboring city, was speaking of it with enthusiasm to some of his friends in one of the public rooms of the hotel where he lived, when a self-conceited ignoramus and moral bully — conspicuous in business and church circles — looking for all the world the incarnation of virtue and wisdom, but who never lost an opportunity of exposing his ignorance — scattered the company as if a bomb had exploded in their midst, by remarking, with the greatest complacency, — "Mr. King, very likely, has traveled amongst the Socrates!" He had heard of the Japanese and Chinese — why not the Socrates!

Thomas Starr King's famous lecture.

Was n't it Madame de Staël who vexed Heine by asking him, "What do you think of Shakespeare?" "She might as well have asked me," wrote the indignant poet afterward, "what I thought of the Uni-

SHAKE-SPEARE.

verse." Blanco White tells that he once possessed a little pocket edition of Shakespeare, in several small volumes, on the margins of which he marked with pencil lines the passages which struck him with admiration. At first a few passages were marked, — some happy phrase, having to him, a foreigner, often more force than to a native of England, was noted. Now and then something that, if it had no other right to particular comment, reminded him of the poets of his own country. Then would come one of those wonderful passages which, expressed in language of the utmost simplicity, reveal secrets of our common nature with almost the effect of magic, and make the whole world akin. Line after line — scene after scene was thus noted, till the margin of almost every page bore traces of his pencil. A friend of James T. Fields said that "reading Cymbeline through a margin of notes is like playing the pianoforte with mittens on;" and she was fond of quoting a remark once dropped in her hearing by a famous actress: "Shakespeare sets his readers' souls on fire with flashes of genius; his commentators follow close behind with buckets of water putting out the flames."

Marking passages.

Cymbeline with notes.

When Bowdler mentioned his scheme of a purified Shakespeare to Dr. Harrington, "No, no, sir," said the old gentleman, "let us, when we have the woodcock, enjoy the little trail (entrails) on the toast."

A reminiscence of Henry Irving's.
"I remember," said Henry Irving, "that at one of the revivals of Shakespearean plays at the Lyceum, a gentleman leaving the theatre was heard to express the opinion that the play was not a bad one; that he thought it might have a tolerable run, but that it would be very much improved by omitting the quotations. The play was Macbeth." Some one told Fields of a pretentious woman who was once heard to say at a dinner-table, that she had "never read Shakespeare's works herself, but had always entertained the highest opinion of him as a man." Which called out M. W., who convulsed the little group by relating

A comical story.
a comical story of venerable Mr. B., who believes unqualifiedly in Boston as not the hub only, but the forward wheels also, of the Universe. The excellent old gentleman, having confessed that he had never found time, during his busy life, to read the "immortal plays," was advised to do so, during the winter then approaching. In the spring G. called on the estimable

citizen, and casually asked if he had read any of the plays during the season just passed. Yes, he replied, he had read them all. "Do you like them?" returned G., feeling his way anxiously to an opinion. "Like them!" replied the old man, with effusive ardor; "that is not the word, sir! They are glorious, sir; far beyond my expectation, sir! There are not twenty men in Boston, sir, who could have written these plays!" "I take an interest, my lord," said Mrs. Wititterly, with a faint smile, "such an interest in the drama." "Ye-es. It's very interasting," replied Lord Frederick Verisopht. "I'm always ill after Shakespeare," said Mrs. Wititterly. "I scarcely exist the next day; I find the reaction so very great after a tragedy, my lord, and Shakespeare is such a delicious creature." "Ye-es!" replied Lord Frederick. "He was a clayver man." On the margin of an old folio copy of Shakespeare's plays was found this note by the poet Keats: "The genius of Shakespeare was an innate universality; wherefore he laid the achievements of human intellect prostrate beneath his indolent and kingly gaze. He could do easily men's utmost. His plan of tasks to come was not of this

Asked if he liked the plays.

Keats' estimate.

world. If what he proposed to do hereafter would not in the idea answer the aim, how tremendous must have been his conception of ultimates!"

PARADOXES. There are truths and facts, so strange and absurd, that, state them how you may, they seem paradoxical. Lieutenant Ray gives some very remarkable experiences in the Arctic region. In excavating the frozen earth he found it harder to work than granite. Powder had no effect whatever upon it, and when a blast was inserted it would always "blow out." The drills used were highly tempered, but in a few hours at farthest the tempering was gone. He found that the extreme cold had the same effect on tempered steel as extreme heat. The steel would lose its temper, become *Observation of De Tocqueville's.* softened, and bend easily. De Tocqueville thought it astonishing that the masses should find their position the more intolerable the more it is improved. It has been remarked upon as curious that Guizot, from whose lectures Mazzini said he first learned to love civil and religious liberty, should have "truckled to the base measures of Louis Philippe." Strange that in Arcadia ninety-five per cent. of the inhabitants should be unable to read and write; that in Venice, a city built upon the water, water to drink should sell for a penny a glass; that the beautiful valleys of Switzerland should be infected with such a disgusting disease as goitre; that in Spain, where all men smoke, and most women, the culture of tobacco should be forbidden by law. It is an historical fact that a fugitive slave was the founder of Virginia. It is believed in England that the famous commodore in the American navy, John Paul Jones, was once horsewhipped by a British officer, — Jones being pronounced a poltroon. In Buckle's note-book is this: "Wrote account of bad emperors favoring Christianity and the good emperors persecuting it." And this: "Began and finished notes of 'Spain' and 'Inquisition,' to prove that morals have not diminished persecution." The Czar (Alexander II.) who emancipated the serfs was assassinated in the name of liberty; and the novelist (Turgenieff) whose humanity was his glory was an exile from his country by the direction of the Emperor (Alexander II.) who admired him and was governed by him in great works, because the liberalism of the author was too much for the

Switzerland and goitre.

Alexander II. and Turgenieff.

imperialism of the Russian system. Trelawny wrote of Shelley after seeing him the first time: "I was silent from astonishment; was it possible this mild-looking, beardless boy could be the veritable monster at war with all the world? — excommunicated by the Fathers of the Church, deprived of his civil rights by the fiat of a grim Lord Chancellor, discarded by every member of his family, and denounced by the rival sages of our literature as the founder of a Satanic school." Yet "we have only to read Shelley's Essays on Christianity," says Symonds, in his biography of the poet, "in order to perceive what reverent admiration he felt for Jesus, and how profoundly he understood the true character of his teaching. That work, brief as it is, forms one of the most valuable extant contributions to a sound theology, and is morally far in advance of the opinions expressed by many who regard themselves as especially qua ified to speak on the subject. It is certain that as Christianity passes beyond its mediæval phase, and casts aside the husk of outworn dogmas, it will more and more approximate to Shelley's exposition. Here and there only is a vital faith, adapted to the conditions

The beardless boy a monster?

A contribution to sound theology.

of modern thought, indestructible because essential, and fitted to unite instead of separating minds of diverse quality. It may sound paradoxical to claim for Shelley of all men a clear insight into the enduring elements of the Christian creed; but it was precisely his detachment from all its accidents which enabled him to discern its spiritual purity, and placed him in a true relation to the Founder. For those who would neither on the one hand relinquish what is permanent in religion, nor yet on the other deny the inevitable conclusions of modern thought, his teaching is indubitably valuable. His fierce tirades against historic Christianity must be taken as directed against an ecclesiastical system of spiritual tyranny, hypocrisy, and superstition, which, in his opinion, had retarded the growth of free institutions, and fettered the human intellect. Like Campanella, he distinguished between Christ, who sealed the gospel of charity with his blood, and those Christians who would be the first to crucify their Lord if he returned to the earth." Doran, in his Table Traits, attributes to a clergyman the accidental invention of bottled ale. Dean Nowell was out fishing, with a bottle of the

A paradoxical claim.

Like Campanella.

freshly-drawn beverage at his side, when intelligence reached him touching the peril his life was in under Mary, which made him fly, after flinging away his rod and thrusting his bottle of ale under the grass. When he could again safely resort to the same spot, he looked for his bottle, which, on being disturbed, drove out the cork like a pellet from a gun, and contained so creamy a fluid, that the dean, noting the fact, and rejoicing therein, took care to be well provided with the same thenceforward. We have it upon the authority of Morley that one of Burke's chief panegyrists, who calls him one of the greatest of men, and, Bacon alone excepted, the greatest thinker who ever devoted himself to the practice of English politics, oddly enough insists upon it that this great man and great thinker was actually out of his mind when he composed the pieces for which he has been most admired and revered. It is curious that the finest sonnet in the English language, in the judgment of Coleridge and other eminent critics, should have been written by a Spaniard. It has been remarked as not a little singular that the house in Cheyne-row, Chelsea, so long the home of Carlyle, the great de-

Origin of bottled ale.

Sonnet, To Night.

nouncer of quacks, should have become the property of a quack medicine proprietor. On her way to prison, one of the officers said to Madame Roland, brutally, "Your husband's flight is a proof of his guilt." She indignantly replied: "It is so atrocious to persecute a man who has rendered such services to the cause of liberty. His conduct has been so open and his accounts so clear, that he is perfectly justifiable in avoiding the last outrages of envy and malice. Just as Aristides, and inflexible as Cato, he is indebted to his virtues for his enemies. Let them satiate their fury upon me. I defy their power, and devote myself to death. He ought to save himself for the sake of his country, to which he may yet do good." Sainte-Beuve characterizes Cowper as essentially the family poet, though he had never been a husband or a father; the poet of the home, of the ordered, pure, softly animated interior, of the grove seen at the bottom of the garden, or of the fireside. Tycho Brahe, afraid of casting a stain upon his nobility by publishing his observations on a new star, did not scruple to debase his lineage by marrying a servant-girl. Hood saw on Sir Thomas Lawrence's easel an unfinished

Madame Roland on her way to prison.

Cowper the family poet.

head of Wilberforce, so very merry, so rosy, so good-fellowish, that nothing less than the Life and Correspondence just published could have persuaded him that he was really a serious character. Peterborough, though an avowed free-thinker, sat up all night at sea, Macaulay tells us, to compose sermons, and was with difficulty prevented from edifying the crew of a man-of-war with his pious oratory. The widow of Nicholas Rowe received a pension from the crown, "in consideration," not of his dramatic genius, but "of the translation of Lucan's Pharsalia." That famous treatise, The Religio Medici, now understood to have been written by Sir Thomas Browne for his own edification, was published surreptitiously by the printer. Fenimore Cooper, in an interview with Sir Charles Murray, who in early life spent a year among the Pawnees, remarked to him, alluding to the publication of The Prairie Bird, "You have had the advantage of me, for I was never among the Indians. All that I know of them is from reading and from hearing my father speak of them. He saw a great deal of the red men when he first went to the western part of the State of New York about the close of the

Peterborough composing sermons.

Cooper never among the Indians.

past century." Bruce, the traveler, was scarcely believed in as a narrator of facts; but he was accepted as a sort of gigantic liar, whose achievements in that way were worthy of respect. An old Scotch lady who knew him said that even in the society in which he was welcome, his African stories were never believed, though the credibility of them has since been abundantly established. "I was present in a large company," said Horace Walpole, "at dinner, when Bruce was talking away. Some one asked him what musical instruments were used in Abyssinia. Bruce hesitated, not being prepared for the question: and at last said, 'I think I saw one lyre there.' George Selwyn whispered his next man, 'Yes; and there is one less since he left the country.'" It is referred to as a curious fact that, although dramatic composition requires more worldly experience and knowledge of human nature than any other, almost all our best comedies have been written by very young men. Those of Congreve were all produced before he was five and twenty. Farquhar composed The Constant Couple in his twenty-second year, and died at thirty. Vanbrugh was a young ensign when he

A truthful traveler accepted as a gigantic liar.

Our best comedies written by young men.

sketched out The Relapse and The Provoked Wife, and Sheridan reached the summit of his dramatic reputation at twenty-six. Haydn thought it unfortunate that circumstances had led him so preponderantly into the field of instrumental composition, rather than into that of operatic writing. Hogarth persisted to the last in believing that the world was in a conspiracy against him with respect to his talents as a historical painter, and that a set of miscreants, as he called them, were employed to run his genius down. When Michel Angelo proposed to fortify his native city, Florence, and was desired to keep to his painting and sculpture, he answered that those were his recreations, but what he really understood was architecture. They say it was Liston's firm belief that he was a great and neglected tragic actor; it is said, too, that every one of us believes in his heart, or would like to have others believe, that he is something which he is not. "At school," said Daniel Webster, "there was one thing I could not do. I could not make a declamation. I could not speak before the school." Boswell said we must not estimate a man's powers by his being able or not able to deliver his sentiments in public. Isaac Hawkins Browne, one of the first wits in Great Britain, got into Parliament, and never opened his mouth. Selwyn, the man renowned for social wit, was utterly deficient in the gift of oratory. He sat forty years in Parliament for Gloucester, and never spoke on any question. Addison, versed in all literature, and so familiar with the oratorical remains of the ancients, is known to have been unable to conclude a speech that he had begun. Dr. Johnson said that Garrick, though accustomed to face multitudes, when produced as a witness in Westminster Hall, was so disconcerted by a new mode of public appearance, that he could not understand what was asked. He told Sir William Scott that he himself had several times tried to speak in the Society of Arts and Sciences, but "had found he could not get on." William Gerard Hamilton told Boswell that Johnson had observed to him that it was prudent for a man who had not been accustomed to speak in public, to begin in as simple a manner as possible a speech which he had prepared; "but," added he, "all my flowers of oratory forsook me." Olivet, in his History of the French Academy, says that La Rochefou-

La Roche-foucauld. cauld could not summon resolution, at his election, to address the Academy. Although chosen a member, he never entered; for such was his timidity, that he could not face an audience and pronounce the usual compliment on his introduction; he whose courage, whose birth, and whose genius were alike distinguished. *Smollett.* Smollett, who malignantly criticised Garrick in Roderick Random and Peregrine Pickle, laboriously panegyrized him in his History, telling him in a letter that "he thought it a duty incumbent on him to make a public atonement, in a work of truth, for the wrongs done him in a work of fiction." *Montesquieu.* It is said of Montesquieu that he was so much affected by the criticisms which he daily experienced that they contributed to hasten his death. *Irving.* The public schools of France, we believe, make use of Irving's Sketch Book as a text-book in English, yet the illustrious author confessed his sufferings from the opinion of a Philadelphia critic, who, on reviewing The Sketch Book, on its first appearance, said that Rip Van Winkle was a silly attempt at humor quite unworthy of the author's genius.

Lamb said, "He who thought it not good for man to be alone preserve me from the more prodigious monstrosity of being never by myself!" Byron said, "All the world are to be at Madame de Staël's to-night, and I am not sorry to escape any part of it. I only go out to get me a fresh appetite for being alone." "In the world," said De Sénancour, "a man lives in his own age; in solitude in all ages." "Conversation," observes Gibbon, "enriches the understanding, but solitude is the school of genius." "Solitude," as Lowell expresses it, "is as needful to the imagination as society is wholesome to the character." "Solitude," says De Quincey, "though silent as light, is, like light, the mightiest of agencies; for solitude is essential to man. All men come into this world alone; all leave it alone. Even a little child has a dread, whispering consciousness, that if he should be summoned to travel into God's presence, no gentle nurse will be allowed to lead him by the hand, nor mother to carry him in her arms, nor little sister to share his trepidations. King and priest, warrior and maiden, philosopher and child, all must walk those mighty galleries alone. How much this fierce condition of

[sidenotes: SOLITUDE. Wholesome to the character.]

eternal hurry upon an arena too exclusively human in its interests is likely to defeat the grandeur which is latent in all men, may be seen in the ordinary effect from living too constantly in varied company. The word dissipation, in one of its uses, expresses that effect; the action of thought and feeling is too much dissipated and squandered. To reconcentrate them into meditative habits, a necessity is felt by all observing persons for sometimes retiring from crowds. No man ever will unfold the capacities of his own intellect who does not at least checker his life with solitude. How much solitude, so much power." Late in life, Sydney Smith wrote: "Living a great deal alone (as I now do) will, I believe, correct me of my faults, for a man can do without his own approbation in much society; but he must make great exertions to gain it when he is alone; without it, I am convinced, solitude is not to be endured." Klopstock, in his Messiah, expresses it: "Solitude holds a cup sparkling with bliss in her right hand, a raging dagger in her left; to the blest she offers her goblet, but stretches towards the wretch the ruthless steel." Julian Hawthorne, writing of his father, says that not even

The ordinary effect of too much company.

How much solitude, so much power.

the author's wife ever saw him in the act of writing. He had to be alone. Years after The Scarlet Letter was published, the author revisited the solitary upper room in which it was written, and entered in his note-book, "In this dismal chamber fame was won." Balzac, when he had thought out one of his philosophical romances, and amassed his materials, retired to his study, and from that time until his book was finished, society saw him no more. When he appeared again among his friends he looked like his own ghost. Lincoln, it is said, had a habit of occasionally spending a whole day by himself in the broad prairie under the blue expanse of heaven, which gave to his face, for a time afterwards, a certain expression of otherworldliness. The only pulpit orator who ever helped me to a conception of the patriarchs and prophets was a circuit-rider who read his Bible in the wilderness. Jesus went up into the mountain alone to pray. Moses was buried in a lost ravine: "angels were his pall-bearers, and God Almighty dug his grave." No man knoweth his sepulchre unto this day.

The Scarlet Letter.

Lincoln.

Moses.

STYLE.

Read, says Southey, all the treatises upon composition that ever were composed, and you will find nothing which conveys so much useful instruction as the account given by John Wesley of his own way of writing. "I never think of my style," says he, "but just set down the words that come first. Only when I transcribe anything for the press, then I think it my duty to see that every phrase be clear, pure, and proper: conciseness, which is now as it were natural to me, brings quantum sufficit of strength. If after all I observe any stiff expression, I throw it out, neck and shoulders." "The ultimate rule is," said Carlyle: "learn so far as possible to be intelligible and transparent — no notice taken of your style, but solely of what you express by it." "Remember," says Cowper, "that, in writing, perspicuity is always more than half the battle. The want of it is the ruin of more than half the poetry that is published. A meaning that does not stare you in the face is as bad as no meaning, because nobody will take the pains to poke for it." "Clear writers, like clear fountains," wrote Landor, "do not seem so deep as they are: the turbid look the most profound." "In composing, as a

Perspicuity more than half the battle.

general rule," advised Sydney Smith, "run your pen through every other word you have written; you have no idea what vigor it will give your style." Bacon, it has been well said, packs his meaning till the plain words take on an air of enigma from their very excess of significance; it is a condensed speech, — a dialect borrowed from the gods. "The best passages in our chief prose writers, no less than in our poets, are where the phraseology has become oracular; the verbiage grows wiser than the thoughts, more tender than the feelings; and the man who falls into this trance of language is himself the most amazed at the glory and the beauty of the utterance." "A style grows from within, and forms only round a nucleus of thought." "Language is part of a man's character." "A good writer does not write as people write, but as he writes." "The sentences of Seneca are stimulating to the intellect; the sentences of Epictetus are fortifying to the character; the sentences of Marcus Aurelius find their way to the soul." Carlyle, in describing the style of Marquis Mirabeau (father of the great Mirabeau), gives a pretty good description of his own: "Marquis Mirabeau had the indisputablest ideas;

[sidenotes: Bacon. / The sentences of Seneca, Epictetus, and Marcus Aurelius.]

but then his style! In very truth, it is the strangest of styles, though one of the richest: a style full of originality, picturesqueness, sunny vigor; but all cased and slated over, threefold, in metaphor and trope; distracted into tortuosities, dislocations; starting out into crotchets, cramp turns, quaintnesses, and hidden satire; which the French had no ear for. Strong meat, too tough for babes!" So it was that England had at first no palate for his own strong, tough meat. He wrote in his Journal: "Literature still all a mystery; nothing 'paying'; Teufelsdröckh beyond measure unpopular. An oldest subscriber came in to Fraser and said, 'If there is any more of that damned stuff, I will, etc., etc.'; on the other hand, an order from America (Boston or Philadelphia) to send a copy of the magazine 'so long as there was anything of Carlyle's in it.'" Napier unexpectedly, and even gratefully, accepted Characteristics, Froude tells us. He confessed that he could not understand it; but anything which Carlyle wrote, he said, had the indubitable stamp of genius upon it, and was therefore most welcome in the Edinburgh Review. Charles Sumner observed to Lord Jeffrey that he thought

The strangest of styles.

Teufelsdröckh.

Characteristics.

Carlyle had changed his style since he wrote the article on Burns. "Not at all," said Jeffrey; "I will tell you why that it is different from the other articles — I altered it." "'T is a good rule of rhetoric," thought Emerson, "which Schlegel gives — 'In good prose every word is underscored'; which, I suppose means, never italicize. Dr. Channing's piety and wisdom had such weight that, in Boston, the popular idea of religion was whatever this eminent divine held. But I remember that his best friend, a man of guarded lips, speaking of him in a circle of admirers, said: 'I have known him long, I have studied his character, and I believe him capable of virtue.' An eminent French journalist paid a high compliment to the Duke of Wellington, when his documents were published: 'Here are twelve volumes of military dispatches, and the word glory is not found in one of them.'" "Right words in right places," was Daniel Webster's idea of style, which he came as near realizing as any one; for even the fastidious Samuel Rogers was free to say that he knew nothing in the English language so well written as Mr. Webster's letter to Lord Ashburton on the subject of the impressment of seamen. Of

A good rule of rhetoric.

Right words in right places.

Montaigne and his style, Emerson says: "The sincerity and marrow of the man reaches to his sentences. I know not anywhere the book that seems less written. It is the language of conversation transferred to a book. Cut these words and they would bleed; they are vascular and alive."

PUBLIC SPEAKING.   Examples without doubt may be cited of great writers who have been illustrious as speakers; but it is a general truth, that to write a book is a bad preparation for public and premeditated speaking. Literary labor, as judiciously observed, is regular and methodical. The writer proposes to himself an ideal perfection, inconsistent with the unforeseen or accidental turn of a debate. Almost all the merits of a book are defects in a speech. A great book is written for the future. A speech is made for the present. Its business is the business of to-day. A book is thought; a speech is action. What is explained in a *Fox's assertion.* book is only hinted at in a debate. Fox asserted that if a speech read well it was not a good speech. A speech is to be heard and not read. Lysias, says Plutarch, wrote a defense for a man who was to be tried before one of the Athenian tribunals. Long before the defendant had learned the speech by heart, he became so much dissatisfied with it that he went in great distress to the author. "I was delighted with your speech the first time I read it; but I liked it less the second time, and still less the third time; and now it seems to be no defense at all." "My good friend," said Lysias, "you quite forget that the judges are to hear it only once." When Dr. Johnson furnished Boswell with the materials for an address to a committee of the House of Commons on an election petition he added, "This you must enlarge on. You must not argue there as if you were arguing in the schools. You must say the same thing over and over again, in different words. If you say it but once, they miss it in a moment of inattention." The masters of eloquence have enforced the rule. It was an axiom of Thiers' that when a speaker wants to carry away a stolid assembly or uncultured mass, he should often present the same argument, but each time in a new verbal dress. Therefore he did not fear repeating himself, but was careful to vary the form of his repetitions. Fox advised Sir Samuel Romilly, when

Dissatisfied with the speech.

Thiers' axiom.

about to sum up the evidence in Lord Melville's trial, "not to be afraid of repeating observations which were material, since it were better that some of the audience should observe it than that any should not understand." Though he himself was censured for the practice, he declared it to be his conviction, from long experience, that the system was right. Pitt urged a similar defense for the amplification which was thought by some to be a defect in his style. "Every person," he said, "who addressed a public assembly, and was anxious to make an impression upon particular points, must either be copious upon those points or repeat them, and that he preferred copiousness to repetition." Lord Brougham gives his testimony on the same side. The orator, he remarks, often feels that he could add strength to his composition by compression, but his hearers would then be unable to keep pace with him, and he is compelled to sacrifice conciseness to clearness. Erskine's great artifice, we are told, lay in his frequent repetitions. He had one or two leading arguments and facts on which he was constantly dwelling. But then he had marvelous skill in varying his phraseology, so that no one was sensible

Pitt's amplification.

Erskine's artifice.

of tautology in the expressions. Like the doubling of a hare, he was perpetually coming to his old place. Landor, in one of his Imaginary Conversations, makes Pericles say to Alcibiades, that, "When we have much to say, the chief difficulty is to hold back some favorite thought, which presses to come on before its time, and thereby makes a confusion in the rest. If you are master of your temper, and conscious of your superiority, the words and thoughts will keep their ranks, and will come into action with all their energy, compactness, and weight. Never attempt to alter your natural tone of voice; never raise it above its pitch: let it at first be somewhat low and slow. This appears like diffidence; and men are obliged to listen the more attentively, that they may hear it. Beginning with attention, they will retain it through the whole speech; but attention is, with difficulty, caught in the course of one." But intense interest and profound feeling are also necessary to effective oratory. An eminent Englishman said to Hawthorne that Sir Lytton Bulwer asked him whether he heard his heart beat when he was going to speak. "Yes." "Does your voice frighten you?"

Pericles to Alcibiades.

Desiderata.

"Yes." "Do all your ideas forsake you?" "Yes." "Do you wish the floor to open and swallow you?" "Yes." "Why, then, you'll make an orator!" The same gentleman told of Canning, too, how once, before rising to speak in the House of Commons, he bade his friends feel his pulse, which was throbbing terrifically. "I know I shall make one of my best speeches," said Canning, "because I'm in such an awful funk!" Pitt did not like to take part in a debate when his mind was full of an important secret of state. "I must sit still," he once said to Lord Shelburne on such an occasion; "for, when once I am up, everything that is in my mind comes out." "In order," says Judge Brackenridge, "to speak short upon any subject — think long. Much reflection is the secret of all that is truly excellent in oratory. No man that speaks just enough, and no more, ever wearies those that hear him. And that is enough which exhausts the subject, before the patience of the auditory." Prince Bismarck once said, "The day will yet come, when what is called eloquence will be regarded as a quality injurious to the state, and punished when it is guilty of a long speech."

Canning.

To speak short, think long.

Of making many books there is indeed no end. It is told of an Oriental king that his library was so large that it required one hundred persons to take care of it, and a thousand dromedaries to transport it. He ordered all useless matter weeded out, and after thirty years' labor it was reduced to the carrying capacity of thirty camels. Still appalled by the number of volumes, he ordered it to be condensed to a single dromedary load, and when the task was completed, age had crept upon him, and death awaited him. Think of "that catholic dome in Bloomsbury," as Thackeray calls the British Museum (to which, it will be recollected, he likened "the dome which held Macaulay's brain"), "under which one million volumes are housed." Dr. Holmes has told how to see the great treasure-house; and what he has said would apply to the books it contains. "Take lodgings," he says, "next door to it,— in a garret, if you cannot afford anything any better,— and pass all your days at the Museum during the whole period of your natural life. At three score and ten you will have some faint conception of the contents, significance, and value of the great British institution." Whitaker's reference

Books and Reading.

That catholic dome in Bloomsbury.

catalogue of current literature alone, published in London, is ten inches thick, and contains over sixty-eight thousand references. One hundred and thirty publishers are represented in it. The preparation of a universal index of subjects, the record of all that human beings have ever written upon anything, an English writer suggests must be left for the German government when it has conquered the world, or for the scion of the Rothschilds, or the Astors, or the Vanderbilts, who is one day to appear, and who to a fortune of twenty millions is to add burning philanthropy and acute bibliomania. In view of the vast quantity of printed matter Schopenhauer urges "the paramount importance of acquiring the art not to read." The library of Voltaire is represented as neither so numerous nor so varied as his fortune and the extent of his knowledge seemed to require. He thought we ought to set bounds to our reading, and that when we had seen a certain number of authors we had seen all. "Books which please for a year, which please for ten years, and which please forever," says Sir James Mackintosh, "gradually take their destined stations." "Posterity," says Matthew Arnold, "alarmed at the way in which its literary baggage grows upon it, always seeks to leave behind it as much as it can, as much as it dares — everything but masterpieces." Emerson says, "There is no luck in literary reputation. They who make up the final verdict upon every book are not the partial and noisy readers of the hour when it appears; but a court as of angels, a public not to be bribed, not to be entreated, and not to be overawed, decides upon every man's title to fame. Only those books come down which deserve to last." Thackeray thought it a comfort that the thousands and thousands of pictures in the Louvre are not all masterpieces, and that there is a good stock of mediocrity in this world, and that we only light upon genius now and then, at rare angel intervals, handed round like Tokay at dessert, in a few houses, and in very small quantities only. Fancy how sick one would grow of it, if one had no other drink. The great books in the great libraries are few indeed in comparison to the whole number, and their condition is proof of how little they are handled by the multitude of readers. Weeding, according to the highest standards, would leave the miles of shelves com-

paratively empty. Jeffrey, in reviewing Campbell's Specimens of the British Poets, published in 1819, says: "Of near two hundred and fifty authors, whose works are cited in these volumes, by far the greater part of whom were celebrated in their generation, there are not thirty who now enjoy *The popular.* anything that can be called popularity — whose works are to be found in the hands of ordinary readers, in the shops of ordinary booksellers, or in the press for republication. About fifty may be tolerably familiar to men of taste or literature; the rest slumber on the shelves of collectors, and are partially known to a few antiquaries and scholars. . . . Now, if this goes on for a hundred years longer, what a task will await the poetical readers of 1919! Our living poets will then be nearly as old as Pope and Swift are at present, but there will stand between them and that gener-
The fresh and fashionable. ation nearly ten times as much fresh and fashionable poetry as is now interposed between us and those writers; and if Scott, and Byron, and Campbell have already cast Pope and Swift a good deal into the shade, in what form and dimensions are they themselves likely to be presented to the eyes of their great-grandchildren? The

thought, we own, is a little appalling; and, we confess, we see nothing better to imagine than that they may find a comfortable place in some new collection of specimens — the centenary of the present publication. There — if the future editor have anything like the indulgence and veneration for antiquity of his predecessor — there shall posterity hang with rapture on the half of Campbell, and the fourth part of Byron, and the sixth of Scott, and the scattered tithes of Crabbe, and the three per cent. of Southey; while some good-natured critic shall sit in our mouldering chair, and more than half prefer them to those by whom they have been superseded." The Tennysons and the Longfellows of the present day must in like manner suffer by new candidates for poetical fame, and so the fashion and taste will ever go on changing — the "immortals" of a thousand years composing a still diminutive list. "It is," says De Quincey, "one of the misfortunes of life that one must read thousands of books only to discover that one need not have read them." "In science," Bulwer suggests, "read, by preference, the newest works; in literature, the oldest. The classic literature is always modern. New books

Nothing better to imagine.

One of the misfortunes of life.

revive and redecorate old ideas; old books suggest and invigorate new ideas." Carlyle speaks of a book that in a high degree excited him to self-activity, which he regarded as the best effect of any book. "The principal use of reading to me," says Montaigne, "is that, by various objects, it rouses my reason; it employs my judgment, not my memory." "The tendency of education through books," says Mark Pattison, "is to sharpen individuality, and to cultivate independence of mind, to make a man cease to be 'the contented servant of the things that perish.' The conversation of the man who reads to any purpose will be flavored by his reading; but it will not be about his reading. The people who read in order to talk about it, are the people who read the books of the season because they are the fashion — books which come in with the season and go out with it. We read books that we may escape from the terrible ennui of society. We go to read, not from craving for excitement, but as a refuge from the tedium vitæ, the irksomeness of herding with uninteresting fellow mortals." The scholar consults books as the mechanic employs his tools. Milton's "industrious and select reading," in prep-

The best effect of any book.

The books that are the fashion.

aration for the great work to which he dedicated a whole life, "long choosing, and late beginning," is as well known as the thirty years spent by Edward Gibbon in preparing for and in composing his history. Carlyle read twenty-five large volumes before he felt himself competent to begin his essay on Diderot, and Dickens felt it necessary to look through with some care the barrow load of French books sent him by Carlyle before beginning his Tale of Two Cities. Then there are big books — huge folios — foundations of great libraries — that are never read or even consulted. The first books given to Dartmouth College, we are told, were of that character. Like the matchlock guns, they could not be held out for use without a rest. There are several hundred volumes of them: two feet long, eighteen inches wide, and six inches thick. An old librarian of the college said the old folios were never read. Those who affected to know more than their classmates took them out. One learned senior told him that he always had three charged to him, one for a footstool, one for a cushion to his chair, and one for his water pail to rest on. "What harm can a book do that costs a hundred crowns?"

Literary preparation.

The old folios never read.

once asked Voltaire. "Twenty volumes folio will never cause a revolution; it is the little portable volumes of thirty sous that are to be feared." The completed Chinese Encyclopædia comprises five thousand and twenty volumes; price seven thousand five hundred dollars. "The crystallized thoughts of the wisest and best of all time, the recorded experiences of men, and the accumulated knowledge of the world, are mighty instruments for living men. One cannot learn everything, but a perfect library must have all the things which books can teach to all men." "By my books," a scholar has said, " I can conjure up to vivid existence before me all the great and good men of antiquity; and for my individual satisfaction I can make them act over again the most renowned of their exploits. The orators declaim for me; the historians recite; the poets sing; in a word, from the equator to the pole, and from the beginning of time until now, by my books, I can fly whither I please." In a letter to Vittori, after giving a humorous description of the manner in which he passed his time in his country-house — snaring thrushes, cutting wood, and playing at cricca and tric-trac with a butcher,

The little volumes feared.

Magical influence of books.

a miller, and two kiln-men, Machiavelli says: "But when evening comes I return home, and shut myself up in my study. Before I make my appearance in it, I take off my rustic garb, soiled with mud and dirt, and put on a dress adapted for courts or cities. Thus fitly habited I enter the antique resorts of the ancients; where, being received, I feed on that food which alone is mine, and for which I was born. For an interval of four hours I feel no annoyance; I forget every grief, I neither fear poverty nor death, but am totally immersed." Lady Mary Wortley Montagu at the age of sixty-two wrote to her daughter: "I give you thanks for your care of my books. I yet retain, and carefully cherish, my taste for reading. If relays of eyes were to be hired like post-horses, I would never admit any but silent companions; they afford a constant variety of entertainment, which is almost the only one pleasing in the enjoyment, and inoffensive in the consequence." At sixty-eight she wrote also to her daughter, "The active scenes are over at my age. I indulge, with all the art I can, my taste for reading. If I would confine it to valuable books, they are almost as scarce as valu-

The antique resorts of the ancients.

A constant variety of entertainment.

able men. I must be content with what I can find. As I approach a second childhood, I endeavor to enter into the pleasures of it. Your youngest son is, perhaps, at this very moment, riding on a poker, with delight, not at all regretting that it is not a gold one, and much less wishing it an Arabian horse, which he could not know how to manage. I am reading an idle tale, not expecting wit or truth in it, and am glad it is not metaphysics to puzzle my judgment, or history to mislead my opinion. He fortifies his health by exercise; I calm my cares by oblivion. The methods may appear low to busy people; but if he improves his strength, and I forget my infirmities, we both attain very desirable ends." That remarkable passage in one of Dickens' stories, in which Harriet Carker is described reading to Alice Brown — who could forget it? She read to the poor woman "the Eternal Book for all the weary and the heavy-laden; for all the wretched, fallen, and neglected of this earth — read the blessed history, in which the blind, lame, palsied beggar, the criminal, the woman stained with shame, the shunned of all our dainty clay, has each a portion, that no human pride, indifference,

Pleasures of second childhood.

The Eternal Book.

or sophistry through all the ages that this world shall last, can take away, or by the thousandth atom of a grain reduce — read the ministry of Him, who, through the round of human life, and all its hopes and griefs, from birth to death, from infancy to age, had sweet compassion for, and interest in, its every scene and stage, its every suffering and sorrow."

Talleyrand said of Châteaubriand that he became deaf when people ceased talking about him. It is well for us, some one has remarked, that we are born babies in intellect. Could we understand half what most mothers say and do to their infants, we should be filled with a conceit of our own importance, which would render us insupportable through life. It was told of a distinguished Englishman of the last generation that, on leaving the university, he was thus addressed by the head of his college: "Mr. Blank, the tutors think highly of you: your fellow-students think highly of you: I think highly of you; but nobody thinks so highly of you as you think of yourself." Recalling the story of the senior wrangler fresh from his triumph, who, entering a theatre at the same

_{VANITY.}

_{Self-conceit.}

time with royalty, fancied that the audience were standing up to do him honor. Richelieu is said to have valued himself much on his personal activity, — for his vanity was as universal as his ambition. A nobleman at the house of Grammont one day found him employed in jumping, and with all the ease and tact of a Frenchman and a courtier, offered to jump against him. He suffered the Cardinal to jump higher, and soon after found himself rewarded by an appointment. Carlyle tells an incident that recalls Rousseau's vanity. He consented to accompany Madame de Genlis to the theatre, stipulating strict incognito; "he would not be seen there for the world." The pit, however, recognized him, but did not cheer him; and this philosopher hurried indignantly from the scene, not because he was discovered, but because he was not applauded. Thackeray was the opposite. " Even when I am reading my lectures," he said, " I often think to myself, 'What a humbug you are,' and I wonder the people don't find it out." He thought the best antidote for self-conceit was for a man to live where he could meet his betters, intellectual and social. But why cure anything so grateful and gra-

Richelieu's vanity.

Rousseau's.

Thackeray the opposite.

In a Club Corner

cious? Vanity, as well said, does indeed wrap a man up like a cloak. It bestows its blessings freely upon the poet striving against general misappreciation; it enables the poor loser in the great battle of life to make himself happy with some trifling success; it softens the bitter pangs of disappointment, and gives fresh strength for new struggles; it prevents resentment, and facilitates the intercourse of society; it can make any man contented with his lot, and lets the poor drudge in the kitchen think without envy of the statesman in the parlor. Who would not be tempted to frequent irritation if he could enjoy that gift for which the poet so foolishly prayed, the gift of seeing himself as others saw him, and recognize his infinitesimal importance in the eyes of his fellows? It is because of the tender illusions of vanity that a man can accept the petty sphere of his own activity for the wider circle of the world, and shut out the annihilating image of the vast forces beyond. It is the safeguard against a depressing fatalism. Vanity has as many virtues as the vaunted panaceas of medical quackery; and were it not for that softening oil, the wheels of life would grate harsh music too discor-

Blessings of vanity.

The safeguard against a depressing fatalism.

dant for mortal ears. Measureless boon! Thank thee, Heaven!

JUSTICE AND MERCY.

It is related that Sir Giles Rooke had once to preside at the trial of a young woman who was charged with having stolen a saw, valued at ten pence, from an old-iron shop. The evidence was clear against her; but it was found that she had committed the offense from the pressure of extreme want. The jury felt the hardship of the case, and the cruelty of punishing with severity an offense committed under such circumstances; and despite the clearness of the evidence, consulted for some little time in doubt together. At length, however, they agreed, and the foreman, rising with evident agitation, delivered

Verdict, Guilty.

their verdict, Guilty. Upon this, Judge Rooke addressed them in the following terms: "Gentlemen of the jury, the verdict which you have given is the very proper verdict; under the circumstances of the case you could have given no other. I perceive the reluctance with which you have given it. The court, sympathizing with you in the unhappy condition of the prisoner, will inflict the lightest punishment the law will allow. The sentence is that the prisoner be fined one shilling, and be discharged; and if she has not one in her possession, I will give her one for the purpose." The audience, jury, and counsel, showed how deeply they were moved by the language of the venerable judge. Early in this century, we are told, it was the custom in Portugal for the Society of Mercy to supply the instruments of punishment for condemned criminals. They were always present at executions, and sometimes provided rotten ropes, which broke with the offender, and when he fell, they covered him with the flag of mercy, and he was out of the reach of the civil power. There is a pretty fable of a Guebre prophet, who was carried by an angel to a spot whence he beheld the place of torment of the wicked, and informed by the angel of the various reasons for the various conditions in which he saw the several sufferers. His attention was at length especially caught by the situation of a man whose whole naked body was surrounded by raging flames, with the single exception of his left foot. "And what," said the prophet to the angel; "what, my lord, is the cause of that particular exception?" "The man whom thou beholdest,"

Society of Mercy.

The place of torment.

returned the angel, "was, in his lifetime, a wicked king. His oppression of his subjects was grievous, and thou seest how he suffereth for his guilt. But, one day, that miserable tyrant (tyrant though he was) walked near to a sheep cote, where it chanced that he saw a lamb tethered to a stake, and was hungering after the remainder of some hay which had been placed near it, but of which it had already consumed all that was within its reach. The wicked prince, feeling upon that occasion one emotion of pity, stretched out his left foot, and pushed the hay within the reach of the lamb. Thou perceivest, then, O prophet, how surely, among all the sons of men, He loveth all his creatures, and how He beareth in mind every act of love which is performed for them. A single act of mercy, bestowed upon a hungry lamb, has saved from the flames of hell the left foot of even a wicked tyrant." There is a Mohammedan version of one of the actions attributed in India to Buddha. One day a dove came flying up to Moses, and begged for protection against a pursuing hawk. And Moses pitied the dove, and let it take refuge in his bosom. But presently up flew the hawk, and charged Moses with

Suffering of a wicked king.

Effect of a single act of mercy.

injustice and cruelty, inasmuch as he had deprived it of the food it was about to give to its hungering little ones. And Moses felt that in acting kindly towards the dove he had acted cruelly towards the hawk. So, in order to reconcile justice with mercy, he cut off from his own body a piece of flesh as large as the dove, and was about to give it to the hawk for its longing little ones, when the hawk cried: "O prophet of God, I am Michael, and what seems to thee a dove is Gabriel. We came to thee under these forms in order to test and to make manifest thy high-mindedness and thy generosity." And then the two seeming birds disappeared. "I have found men more kind than I expected, and less just," said Dr. Johnson, at the close of his wide experience of life; and the remark would be echoed, we suppose (says an English writer), by every one whose experience or whose anticipations have not been peculiar. Almost every one, we think, has at least once in his life felt that he came in contact with a just mind, — that his shortcomings were estimated without exaggeration, his offenses visited with no more than their merited penalty. If he ask himself what hand has administered this tonic to

Reconciling justice with mercy.

Coming in contact with a just mind.

fainting self-esteem, this anodyne to the flutterings of a restless vanity, he will invariably find, we believe, that it was that of one whose ideal was something different from justice. We do not believe that any human being ever impressed another with the sense of justice, in the face of any real difficulty or obstacle, who was otherwise than boundlessly forgiving. Think of all that a great patriot must condone in his supporters, during a death-struggle with a mighty foe. One shudders to imagine all that must have been permitted, for instance, by a William the Silent. "Charity," says Ruskin, at his best, "is the summit of justice — it is the temple of which justice is the foundation. But you can't have the top without the bottom; you cannot build upon charity. You must build upon justice, for this main reason, that you have not, at first, charity to build with. It is the last reward of good work. Do justice to your brother (you can do that, whether you love him or not), and you will come to love him. But do injustice to him, because you don't love him, and you will come to hate him."

Marginalia: Something different from justice. You can't have the top without the bottom.

It is certain that Richard Brinsley Sheridan will always be an interesting character to attentive readers and students of English literature. Orators, dramatists, playwrights, statesmen, enlightened men and women of the world, close students of human nature, will be particularly interested in him, for the reason, that the development of extraordinary powers, and the notable achievements of genius, must ever and everywhere be engaging to thoughtful people.

<small>SHERIDAN.</small>

It is not often that traits can be traced so unmistakably to progenitors as in the case of Sheridan. His grandfather was a clergyman, but lost his chaplaincy and all hope of further preferment by preaching a sermon on the birthday of George I. from the text: "Sufficient unto the day is the evil thereof." He died, as stated, in great poverty and distress, having maintained through all the changes of fortune a gay and careless cheerfulness, not allowing a day to pass, according to Lord Cork, "without a rebus, an anagram, or a madrigal." He published translations of Greek and Latin classics, and wrote letters, many of which were held of sufficient consequence to be included in Swift's Miscel-

<small>*Traits of progenitors.*</small>

lanies. His father was an actor, an elocutionist, and a lexicographer. He played at Drury Lane, and was set up, we are told, by his friends as a rival to Garrick. One of his published works was a life of his godfather, Jonathan Swift, with whom his father must have been intimate. His mother was a novelist of considerable distinction, her romances still retaining a respectable place in English literature. The distinguishing traits of his grandfather, his father, and his mother, were developed and stimulated by his attachment to Miss Linley, a young and beautiful singer, in defense of whom he fought two duels, to whom he was afterwards married, and by whom his subsequent life was greatly determined.

"He said his wife should sing in public no more, and she did not. In a few years he had written the most brilliant comedies produced since the time of Shakespeare. A few years later he delivered the most electrifying speech ever heard in the House of Commons. He was in Parliament thirty years, and manager of Drury Lane for about the same period. When George IV. was Prince of Wales, Sheridan was his most intimate friend and adviser, shaping, no doubt, the future whisper of the throne.

His father set up as a rival to Garrick.

Summary.

Sheridan was almost a Republican in politics. He stood by the French Revolutionists, by Ireland, and the oppressed myriads of India. He held during his life but two or three offices, and made no money in public affairs. Against these merits and achievements is placed the fact that he made a multitude of engagements and kept but few of them; that he was generally in straits for money; and that he drank at times more port than was good for him. The real moral of his life seems to be that without a sense of order the most versatile genius will be continually in hot water. Sheridan could raise large sums of money for Drury Lane, and manage it through its golden age, yet he allowed small creditors to swarm around him as if helpless. Later in life he settled fifteen thousand pounds upon his second wife, and met with a heavy financial disaster when Drury Lane burned. Yet his debts after death amounted to only four thousand pounds. Such a bankrupt would not amount to a third rate in these days."

Made no money in public affairs.

Debts only four thousand pounds.

From being regarded at school as "a most impenetrable dunce," he rose to be, in many respects, one of the most distinguished men in the world. "The other night," writes Byron, in his Diary, "we were all delivering our respective and various opinions upon Sheridan, and mine was this: 'Whatever Sheridan has done or chosen to do has been par excellence always the best of its kind. He has written the best comedy (School for Scandal); the best opera, The Duenna (in my mind far before that St. Giles's lampoon, The Beggars' Opera); the best farce (the Critic — it is only too good for a farce); and the best address (Monologue on Garrick); and, to crown all, delivered the very best oration (the famous Begum speech) ever conceived or heard in England.' Somebody told Sheridan this, the next day, and, on hearing it, he burst into tears." The speech on the impeachment of Warren Hastings, Burke declared to be "the most astonishing effort of eloquence, argument, and wit, united, of which there was any record or tradition." Fox said, "all that he had ever heard, all that he had ever read, when compared with it, dwindled into nothing, and vanished like vapor before the sun;" and Pitt acknowledged "that it surpassed all the eloquence of ancient and modern times, and possessed everything that genius or art could furnish, to agitate and control the human mind." At the close of it occurs this celebrated passage: "Justice I have now before me, august and pure; the abstract idea of all that would be perfect in the spirits and the aspirings of men! — where the mind rises, where the heart expands — where the countenance is ever placid and benign — where her favorite attitude is to stoop to the unfortunate — to hear their cry and to help them, to rescue and relieve, to succor and save: — majestic from its mercy; venerable from its utility; uplifted without pride; firm without obduracy; beneficent in each preference; lovely, though in her frown!" *Picture of Justice.*

The speech occupied five hours and a half in the delivery. An anecdote is given as a proof of its irresistible power in a note upon Bissett's History of the Reign of George III.: "The late Mr. Logan, well known for his literary efforts, and author of a most masterly defense of Mr. Hastings, went that day to the House of Commons, prepossessed for the accused and against the accuser. At the expiration of the first hour he said to a friend, 'All this is declamatory assertion without proof;' — when the second was finished, 'This is a most *Power of his eloquence.*

wonderful oration;'—at the close of the third, 'Mr. Hastings has acted very unjustifiably;'—the fourth, 'Mr. Hastings is a most atrocious criminal;'—and, at last, 'Of all monsters of iniquity, the most enormous is Warren Hastings.'"

Speech at Westminster Hall. The next year occurred his great speech at Westminster Hall—"the great hall of William Rufus, the hall which had resounded with acclamations at the inauguration of thirty kings"—which lasted four days.

His carelessness and dilatoriness were proverbial. Sir Jonah Barrington, in a note to one of his Personal Sketches, says: "I had an opportunity of knowing that Mr. Sheridan was offered one thousand pounds for his speech in the Warren Hastings case by a bookseller the day after it was spoken in the House of Commons, provided he would write it out correctly from the notes taken, before the interest had subsided; and yet, although he certainly had occasion for money at the time, and assented to the *Delay in writing it out.* proposal, he did not take the trouble of writing a line of it. The publisher was of course displeased, and insisted on his performing his promise, upon which Sheridan laughingly replied in the vein of Falstaff:

'No, Hal, were I at the strappado, I would do nothing by compulsion.' He did, however, write it out at length, but too late, and got nothing for it."

An incident in keeping with this occurred just as he was parting with an acquaintance. "I wrote you a letter," said Mr. Smyth; "it was an angry one; you will be so good as to think no more of it." "Oh, certainly not, my dear Smyth," said Sheridan; "I shall never think of what you have said in it, be assured;" and putting his hand in his pocket, "Here it is," he cried, offering it to Smyth, who was glad enough to get hold of it; and looking at it as he was going to throw it into the fire, lo and behold, he saw that it had never been opened! *Mr. Smyth's letter.*

Sheridan's solicitor found his client's wife one day walking up and down in her drawing-room, apparently in a frantic state of mind. He inquired of Mrs. Sheridan the cause of such violent perturbation. She only replied that her husband was a "villain." On the man of business further interrogating her as to what had so suddenly awakened her to a sense of that fact, she at length answered with some hesitation: "Why, I have discovered that all the *Mrs. Sheridan's perturbation.*

love-letters he sent me were the very same as those which he sent to his first wife!"

The versatility of his genius and his extraordinary knowledge of human nature and of human affairs naturally made him hesitate in his written performances. In his preface to The Rivals he says: "On subjects on which the mind has been much informed, invention is slow of exerting itself. Faded ideas float in the fancy like half-forgotten dreams; and the imagination in its fullest enjoyments becomes suspicious of its offspring, and doubts whether it has created or adopted."

From his preface to The Rivals.

The history of The School for Scandal is a curious one. The play was written piecemeal, and in great haste, having been announced before the parts were delivered to the players. Moore, speaking of the original manuscript, says that the last five scenes were roughly scribbled on odd scraps of paper, the last leaf bearing the inscription in Sheridan's writing of "Finished, thank God," with the prompter's addendum, "Amen. W. Hopkins." No printed copies of the play, authenticated by the author, are in existence. All was thought out carefully in Sheridan's mind before paper was blotted. One of his sis-

School for Scandal "finished."

ters tells that his phrase at home was, "The comedy is finished; I have now nothing to do but to write it." The entire work has been pronounced an El Dorado of wit, where the precious metal is thrown about by all classes as carelessly as if they had not the least idea of value.

El Dorado of wit.

The great success of the play was an astonishment to him, if not something of a terror. "Walking along Piccadilly with Sheridan," says Kelly, "I asked him if he had told the queen that he was writing another play. He said he had, and was actually about one. 'Not you,' said I to him; 'you will never write again; you are afraid to write.' 'Of whom am I afraid?' said he, fixing his penetrating eye on me. I said, 'You are afraid of the author of The School for Scandal.'"

Sheridan was very particular as to how his plays should be represented. In The Memoirs of Charles Mathews, by his wife, is an interesting illustration. Mathews was to play Sir Peter Teazle, in The School for Scandal. Sheridan, then proprietor of Drury Lane theatre, expressed his desire to Mr. Mathews that he would allow the author to read the part to him, and give his idea of the manner he thought that Sir

Particular as to the representation of his plays.

Peter Teazle should be acted. Mathews had many misgivings on this subject, and most embarrassing it proved in the result; for so totally unlike was Sheridan's reading of the character from every other conception of it, that it was next to impossible for the actor to adopt any one of his suggestions. Had it not been known that Sheridan was the author of the play, it would have been difficult to credit his acquaintance with the part in question. The consequence may be anticipated. Sheridan was dissatisfied with Mathews' performance, and the part was given to another.

Sheridan's reading.

There are many anecdotes told, illustrating his extravagance and carelessness in money matters. His brother said that he once found the window frames stuffed with papers to prevent them from rattling, and, on taking them out, saw that they were bank-notes, which Sheridan had used for this purpose some stormy night and never missed them. Sheridan made his appearance one day in a new pair of boots. These attracting the notice of some of his friends — "Now guess," said he, "how I came by these boots?" Many probable guesses then were made. "No," said

Novel use of bank-notes.

Sheridan, "you have not hit it, and never will: I bought them and paid for them." On another occasion it is said he was very much distressed for a pair of boots, and had not money enough to pay for them. He sent his servant to a shoemaker's shop to tell them to send his master a pair of boots. When the boots came, Sheridan complained (like Lord Foppington) "that the right boot pinched him execrably," and ordered him to take it back, leaving the left boot behind. He then sends his servant to another shoemaker's, and serves him the same trick; only sent the left boot back. He thus got a pair of boots, and left his servant to settle the matter with the shoemakers. A friend remonstrating with him, when he was living in Orchard Street, on the extravagance of his establishment, and the smallness of his means to support it, he said, "My dear friend, it is my means." On being asked what wine he liked best, he replied, "Other people's." He told Lord North he had taken a new house, and that everything would now go on like clock-work. "Ah," replied his lordship, "tick, tick." He jocularly remarked one day to a creditor who demanded instant payment of a long stand-

In distress for boots.

"Tick, tick."

ing debt with interest: "My dear sir, you know it is not my interest to pay the principal; nor is it my principle to pay the interest."

Grief for his wife. His grief for his wife was in sharp contrast with his gayety and carelessness. "I never," says Michael Kelly, the famous music composer and singer, "I never beheld more poignant grief than Mr. Sheridan felt for the loss of his beloved wife; and although the world, which knew him only as a public man, will perhaps scarcely credit the fact, I have seen him, night after night, sit and cry like a child, while I sang to him, at his desire, a pathetic little song of my own composition, They Bore Her to Her Grassy Grave."

From all accounts he must have been a great talker. "Poor dear Sherry!" exclaims Byron; "I shall never forget the day he, and Rogers, and Moore, and I, *His conversation.* passed together; when he talked and we listened, without one yawn, from six till one in the morning."

It is said that he never spoke well until after he had drank a couple of bottles of port. Father O'Leary said, "This was like a porter; he could not get on without a load on his head." When he wrote, he always drank. "A glass of wine," he used to say, "would encourage the bright thought to come; and then it was right to take another to reward it for coming." He told Byron that on the night of the grand success of his School for Scandal, he was knocked down and put into the watch-house, for making a row in the street, and being found intoxicated by the watchman. Everybody has heard of his answer to the watchman who found him bereft of that "divine particle of air," called reason. "He, the watchman," says Byron, "found Sherry in the street, fuddled and bewildered, and almost insensible. "Who are you, sir?"— no answer. "What's your name?" — a hiccough. "What's your name, I say?" Answer, in a slow, deliberate, and impressive tone, "Wilberforce!"

On the night of the grand success.

When somebody asked Sheridan how it was he succeeded so well in the house, he replied, "Why, sir, I had not been there very long before I found three fourths of the members were fools, and the whole loved a joke. I resolved, therefore, not to shock them by too much severity of argument, and to amuse them by a sufficient quantity of humor. This is the whole

Why he succeeded in the House of Commons.

secret of my success." Once, being on a parliamentary committee, he arrived when all the members were assembled and seated, and about to commence business. He looked round in vain for a seat, and then, with a bow and a quaint twinkle in his eyes, said, "Will any gentleman move, that I might take the chair?" During the year 1806, having been told that his enemies took pleasure in speaking ill of him, on account of his favoring an obnoxious tax which his party was about to force through the house, — "Well, let them," he said; "it is but fair that they should have some pleasure for their money." Some mention having been made in his presence of a tax upon milestones, he said, "Such a tax would be unconstitutional, as they are a race that cannot meet to remonstrate."

One of his sallies.

The saying ascribed to Sheridan, when seated at the window, a few days before his death, and seeing a hearse go by, he exclaimed, "Ah, that is the carriage, after all!" was in everybody's mouth, and compared with the slow-coach joke of Rogers, who, when told that it was called the "Regulator," remarked, "I thought so, for all the others go by it."

Another.

He was disputing one day with Monk Lewis, the author of The Castle Spectre, which had filled the exhausted treasury of Drury Lane, when the latter, in support of his argument, offered to bet Sheridan all the money The Castle Spectre had brought that he was right. "No," answered the manager; "I cannot afford to bet so much as that; but I will tell you what I will do — I'll bet you all it's worth."

The Castle Spectre.

Lord Lauderdale, happening to say that he would repeat some good things of Sheridan's, he replied, "Pray, don't, my dear Lauderdale; a joke in your mouth is no laughing matter."

Being asked, "Why do we honor ambition and despise avarice, while they are both but the desire of possessing?" "Because," said Sheridan, "the one is natural, the other artificial; the one the sign of mental health, the other of mental decay; the one appetite, the other disease."

Rogers once said to him, "Your admiration of Mrs. Siddons is so high, that I wonder you never made open love to her." "To her!" exclaimed Sheridan; "to that magnificent and appalling creature; I should as soon think of making love to the Archbishop of Canterbury."

Mrs. Siddons.

One day he met two royal dukes in St. James Street, and the younger flippantly remarked, "I say, Sherry, we have just been discussing whether you are a greater fool or rogue: what is your opinion, old boy?" Sheridan bowed, smiled, and, as *Reply to the two royal dukes.* he took each of them by the arm, replied, "Why, faith, I believe I am between both."

Haydon, the painter, says that once, when Sheridan was dining at Somerset House, and they were all in fine feather, the servant rushed in, exclaiming, "Sir, the house is on fire!" "Bring another bottle of claret," said Sheridan; "it is not my house."

GARRICK. One can hardly think of Garrick without thinking also of Dr. Johnson. The great actor and the great moralist are so connected that it is difficult to disassociate them. They were friends for more than forty years, and for most of that time they were intimate. The latter kept a private school at Edial Hall, and the former was one of his three pupils. They went up to London together, without money or friends, to force their fortunes. Garrick fixed upon the law, but poverty interrupted his studies. Receiving a legacy from an uncle, he commenced business with his brother as a wine merchant. Foote used to say, by way of derision, that he remembered Garrick living in Durham-yard, with three quarts of vinegar in the cellar calling himself a wine merchant. He did not continue in the trade long, for we find him persevering in his attendance upon the theatre, writing theatrical criticisms, practicing declamation, and soon making his appearance as an actor, taking the name of Lyddal.

Foote's satire.

His genius for mimicry began to display itself at a very early age. At eleven, we are told, he acted in a play, The Recruiting Officer, before a select audience, with great applause. As manager of the company, he applied to Johnson for a prologue, without success. Afterwards the future colossus of literature was a favorite subject for his mimicry. Funny it must have been to the boys of the little school at Edial to see the future great actor, whose death, Johnson said, "eclipsed the gayety of nations, and impoverished the stock of harmless pleasures," take off "the tumultuous and awkward fondness" of their master for "Tetty" or "Tetsey," as he called his wife, — who was fat, fifty, and anything but pretty.

Genius for mimicry.

Taking off Johnson.

He rose very rapidly in his profession. In a year or two he was famous. His natural acting charmed a public weary, as was said, of the rant and affectation of Macklin or Quin. "Garrick, Madam," said Dr. Johnson to Mrs. Siddons, "was no declaimer; there was not one of his own scene-shifters who could not have spoken To be, or not to be, better than he did; yet he was the only actor I ever saw whom I could call a master both in tragedy and comedy. A true conception of character, and natural expression of it, were his distinguished excellences." It has been said, of all the men of his time, he is the man whom one would perhaps most willingly have seen, because the gifts which threw not only Englishmen, but Frenchmen like Diderot, and Germans like Lichtenberg, into amazement and ecstasy, are exactly those gifts which literary description can do least to reproduce. Burke said that he was the acutest observer of nature that he had ever known.

His natural acting.

A master.

Burke's tribute.

Garrick had a brother living in the country, who was an idolatrous admirer of his genius. A rich neighbor, a grocer, being about to visit London, this brother insisted on his taking a letter of introduction to the actor. Not being able to make up his mind to visit the great man the first day, the grocer went to the play in the evening, and saw Garrick in Abel Drugger. On his return to the country, the brother eagerly inquired respecting the visit he had been so anxious to bring about. "Why, Mr. Garrick," said the good man, "I am sorry to hurt your feelings, but there's your letter. I did not choose to deliver it." "Not to deliver it!" exclaimed the other, in astonishment. "I happened to see him when he did not know me, and I saw that he was such a dirty, low-lived fellow, that I did not like to have anything to do with him." *In Abel Drugger.*

So prodigious was his fame that the great Mr. Pope was drawn from his retreat at Twickenham to see him; and Lord Orrery was so struck with his performance that he said, "I am afraid the young man will be spoiled, for he will have no competitor." Hogarth saw him in Richard III., and on the following night in Abel Drugger: he was so struck, that he said to Garrick, "You are in your element, when you are begrimed with dirt, or up to your elbows in blood." Quin, in his sarcastic vein, said: "This is the wonder of a day; *Hogarth's judgment.*

Garrick is a new religion; the people follow him as another Whitefield; but they will soon return to Church again."

A mute's laudation.

A Mr. Shireff, a deaf and dumb man, was asked, "Did you know Garrick?" "Yes," the man replied, in his own way. "Did you ever see him act?" "Yes," was the reply again. "Did you admire him?" "Yes." "How could that be, when you could not hear him, and, of course, could not understand him?" The answer, when it came, was astonishing indeed: "Garrick's face was a language!"

Garrick's face.

He must have been a trying sitter to the painters. A story is told of the way he tried the patience and temper of Gainsborough. He paid sixteen visits to the artist's studio, and on each occasion had imperceptibly wrought a change in his features; at last the painter, declaring he could not paint a man with such a "Protean phiz," threw down his brush in despair. Macaulay says: "I have seen several pictures of Garrick, none resembling another; and I have heard Hannah More speak of the extraordinary variety of countenances by which he was distinguished."

Pictures all different.

Boswell, referring to Garrick's fame, said he was assuming the airs of a great man.

Johnson said, "Sir, it is wonderful how little Garrick assumes. Consider, sir; celebrated men, such as you have mentioned, have had their applause at a distance; but Garrick had it dashed in his face, sounded in his ears, and went home every night with the plaudits of a thousand in his cranium. Then, sir, Garrick did not find, but made his way to the tables, the levees, and almost to the bed-chambers of the great." Johnson would attack, and almost abuse, Garrick, but he would permit no one else to do so — especially to speak of him apologetically. He once said to Boswell, with a stern look, "Sir, I have known David Garrick longer than you have known him; and I know no right you have to talk to me on the subject."

Applause dashed in his face.

Foote, being notoriously lavish with his money, was fond of taking off Garrick's reputed niggardliness. At the Chapter Coffee-house, Foote and his friends were making a contribution for the relief of a poor fellow, a decayed player, who was nicknamed the Captain of the Four Winds, because his hat was torn into four spouts. Each person of the company dropped his mite into the hat, as it was held out to him. "If Garrick hears of this," ex-

Reputed niggardliness.

claimed Foote, "he will certainly send us his hat." He had a small bust of Garrick placed upon his bureau. "You may be surprised," said he, "that I allow him to be so near my gold; but you will observe he has no hands." Foote and Garrick were leaving the Bedford one night when Foote had been the entertainer, and on his pulling out his purse to pay the bill, a guinea dropped. Impatient at not immediately finding it, "Where on earth can it be gone to?" he said. "Gone to the devil, I think," rejoined Garrick, who had sought for it elsewhere. "Well said, David," cried Foote; "let you alone for making a guinea go farther than anybody else."

Foote's jokes.

Johnson said, when some one present accused Garrick of penuriousness, "Garrick, sir, has given away more money than any man in England that I am acquainted with, and that not from ostentatious views. Garrick was very poor when he began life; so, when he came to have money, he probably was very unskillful in giving away, and savĕd when he should not. But Garrick began to be liberal as soon as he could."

Johnson's retort.

They had much to say about his vanity, especially those who were envious of him. It is said that a gentleman of the law, who could not miss an opportunity of laughing at the great actor's vanity, met him one day, and told him he had been applied to by the booksellers to publish an edition of the Statutes at Large, and he hoped he should find a snug niche in them to introduce him. At a dinner at Thrale's, a gentleman attacked Garrick for being vain. Johnson said, "No wonder, sir, that he is vain; a man who is perpetually flattered in every mode that can be conceived. So many bellows have blown the fire, that one wonders he is not by this time become a cinder."

As to the great actor's vanity.

"It was in Lear's madness," as Murphy observes, "that Garrick's genius was remarkably distinguished. He had no sudden starts, no violent gesticulation; his movements were slow and feeble; misery was depicted in his countenance; he moved his head in the most deliberate manner; his eyes were fixed, or, if they turned to any one near him, he made a pause, and fixed his look on the person after much delay; his features at the same time telling what he was going to say, before he uttered a word. During the whole time, he presented a sight of woe and misery, and a total alienation of mind from every idea

His genius in Lear's madness.

but that of his unkind daughters. He was used to tell how he acquired the hints that guided him, when he began to study this great and difficult part: he was acquainted with a worthy man, who lived in Leman Street, Goodman's Fields; this friend had an only daughter about two years old; he stood at his dining-room window, fondling the child, and dandling it in his arms, when it was his misfortune to drop the infant into a flagged area, where it died instantly. He remained at his window screaming in agonies of grief. The neighbors flocked to the house, took up the child, and delivered it dead to the unhappy father, who wept bitterly, and filled the street with lamentations. He lost his senses, and from that moment never recovered his understanding. As he had a sufficient fortune, his friends chose to let him remain in his house, under two keepers appointed by a physician. Garrick frequently went to see his distracted friend, who passed the remainder of his life in going to the window, and there playing in fancy with his child. After some dalliance, he dropped it, and, bursting into a flood of tears, filled the house with shrieks of grief and bitter anguish. He then sat down in a pensive

Hints that guided him in the part.

His distracted friend.

mood, his eyes fixed on one object, at times looking slowly round him, as if to implore compassion. Garrick was often present at this scene of misery, and was ever after used to say, that it gave him the first idea of King Lear's madness."

The great actor was extremely sensitive. *Sensitiveness.* His great sensibility made him fear, defer to, and ever ready to conciliate the public. "When he first acted Macbeth," Davies tells us, "he was so alarmed with the fears of critical examination, that during his preparation for the character, he devoted some part of the time to the writing of a humorous pamphlet upon the subject. He knew that his manner of representing Macbeth would be essentially different from that of all the actors who had played it for twenty or thirty years before, and he was therefore determined to attack himself ironically, to blunt, if not to prevent, the remarks of others. This pamphlet was *A curious pamphlet.* called 'An Essay on Acting; in which will be considered the mimical Behavior of a certain fashionable faulty Actor, and the Laudableness of such unmanly, as well as inhuman Proceedings; to which will be added, A Short Criticism on his acting Macbeth.' It had this motto on the title-page: 'Macbeth has murdered Garrick.'"

Stage feeling. His extreme sensibility was not inconsistent with his stage feeling. It is recorded of him, that whilst he was drowning the house in tears, in the fourth act of Lear, he put his tongue in his cheek, and said to King, during the applause, "D—n me, Tom, it will do, it will do." It made him painfully dread ridicule. On one occasion, it is said, Quin went to the pit to see his rival act. It was at a time when Hogarth's Marriage a la Mode was familiar to every one. One of the prints of that series represents a negro boy bringing in the tea things. When Garrick, with his diminutive figure and blackened face, came forward as Othello, Quin exclaimed, "Here is Pompey, but where is the tray?" The effect was electrical, and Garrick never attempted Othello again.

Foote and Garrick. Foote was gigantic, as Garrick was diminutive in stature. The former was audacious and aggressive in manner, the latter good-natured, vivacious, and deferential; but he could defend himself. We are told of how a project of Foote's to publicly ridicule Garrick fell through in a singular manner. The parties met, as if by accident, at the house of a nobleman, the common friend of both ; when alighting at the same time from their chariots at his lordship's door, and exchanging significant looks at each other, Garrick broke silence first by asking, "Is it war or peace?" *War or peace?* "Oh! peace, by all means," replied Foote, with apparent good will, and the two spent the day amicably together.

Davies states that after Mr. Garrick had been abroad about a year and a half, satiated with the amusements and pleasures of the continent, he turned his thoughts towards his native country. But before he would set out for Calais, he was resolved to put in practice his usual method of preventing censure, and blunting the edge of ridicule, by anticipation. For this purpose, before he left Paris, he sat down very seriously to write a kind of satirical poem on himself; it was called The Sick Monkey, *The Sick Monkey.* and the plan of it was, the talk or censure of other animals and reptiles on him and his travels, etc. This poem he sent from Paris to a friend, with a request that he would have it printed, to prepare for his reception in London. It attracted little attention, and died almost still-born.

He had intuitively perceived what was

The world likes change. soon to take place. The world likes change. The play-goers of London got tired even of Garrick. It is related as a fact, that one night the cash receipts of Drury Lane, though Garrick and Mrs. Cibber performed in the same play, amounted to no more than three pounds, fifteen shillings, and sixpence!

On Giving Advice. The wise do not need counsel, and fools will not take it, is one of the pregnant sentences of Seneca. And what, to say truth, is more difficult than counsel in the conduct of life? Right and wrong, says Manzoni, never are divided with so clean a cut, that one party has the whole of either. To give advice, as to do good, we must know how to do it; and, like everything else, we can only know this through the medium of our own passions, our own judgment, our own ideas; which not unfrequently are rather as correct as they are capable of being, than as they ought to be. *Goethe to Eckermann.* "When one has looked about him in the world long enough," said Goethe to Eckermann, "to see how the most judicious enterprises frequently fail, and the most absurd have the good fortune to succeed, he becomes disinclined to give any one advice. At bottom, he who asks advice shows himself limited; he who gives it gives also proof that he is presumptuous. If any one asks me for good advice, I say, I will give it, but only on condition that you will promise not to take it." "I have always hated to give advice," says Hawthorne, in the same strain, "especially when there is a prospect of its being taken. It is only one-eyed people who love to advise, or have any spontaneous promptitude of action. When a man opens both his eyes, he generally sees about as many reasons for acting in any one way as in any other, and quite as many for acting in neither; and is therefore likely to leave his friends to regulate their own conduct, and also to remain quiet as regards his especial affairs till necessity shall prick him onward. Nevertheless, the world and individuals flourish upon a constant succession of blunders." "Why do you so much admire the Helen of Zeuxis?" said Nicostratus. "You would not wonder why I so much admired it," replied the painter, "if you had my eyes." Once when Giotto, a friend of Dante, had been summoned to Naples by King Robert, and was executing some paintings for that sov-

One-eyed people.

A succession of blunders.

ereign, the king remarked to him: "Giotto, if I were in your place, now that the weather is so hot, I would give up painting for a time, and take my rest." "And so I would do, certainly," replied Giotto, "if I were in your place." "To look on things like a philosopher," says Molière, "there's nothing occurs to me more fantastical and more impertinent than for one man to pretend to cure another."

Giotto to the king.

LIMITS.   There are limits to everything human. Emerson's stumbling-block at college was mathematics. There is authority for the story that at a late period in life he unwittingly cheated a poor Irishman, while paying him for some work, by calculating that seven times seven were twenty-seven, and the error was not detected until Pat, who had doubts about the matter, consulted a neighbor and came back for a settlement. At Drury Lane theatre the most important novelty from Henderson was King John; and in the great scene with Hubert, his deep smothered undertones had a terrible effect upon those near enough to enjoy the cunning of the scene. The distant auditor complained, as will constantly be the case in theatres of any size, unless a mode of

A scene in King John.

utterance be adopted by the actor, removed very far from the natural elevation or usual articulation of the voice. As we think, says Dr. Holmes, the same thing over many millions of times, and as many persons keep up their social relations by the aid of a vocabulary of only a few hundred words, or, in the case of some very fashionable people, a few scores only, a very limited amount of thinking material may correspond to a full set of organs of sense, and a good development of the muscular system. The author of Lothair makes Pinto exclaim, "English is an expressive language, but not difficult to master. Its range is limited. It consists, as far as I observe, of four words: 'nice,' 'jolly,' 'charming,' and 'bore;' and some grammarians add, 'fond.'" Our language, it is estimated, contains about one hundred and twenty-five thousand words; yet, remarks an English writer, of this immense number it is surprising how few are in common use. I have seen it stated on scholarly authority that a child does not commonly use more than a hundred words; and, unless he belongs to a cultivated family, he will never habitually employ more than three or four hundred. An American

Our limited vocabulary.

The few words in common use.

scholar estimates that few practical writers or speakers use as many as ten thousand words in threescore years of public life. Speakers employ not so many by a large count as writers employ. Max Müller says that "a well educated person that has been at a public school in England and at an English university, who reads his Bible and Shakespeare, and all the books in Mudie's Library — that is, nineteen twentieths of all the books published in England — seldom uses more than three or four thousand words in actual conversation." Eloquent speakers, he thinks, may rise to a command of ten thousand. "Even Milton," writes another critic, "Milton, whose wealth of words seems amazing, and whom Dr. Johnson charges with using a Babylonish dialect, uses only about eight thousand; and Shakespeare, the 'myriad-minded,' only fifteen thousand." The Old Testament contains less by some hundreds than six thousand words.

Writers employ more words.

Milton uses eight thousand.

ON WORKING OURSELVES UP.

"What did you say?" cried Mrs. Joe Gargery, beginning to scream. "What did you say? What did that fellow say to me, Pip? What did he call me, with my husband standing by? O! O! O!" Each of these exclamations was a shriek ; and Pip remarks of his sister, what is equally true of all the violent women he had ever seen, that passion was no excuse for her, because it was undeniable that instead of lapsing into passion, she consciously and deliberately took extraordinary pains to force herself into it, and became blindly furious by regular stages. The full grown Goojerat, or maneless lion of South Africa, is furnished with a rudimentary claw at the end of his tail. This little appendage was supposed by the ancients to be instrumental in lashing the animal into fury, and Mr. Gordon Cumming says that the natives believe it to be the residence of an evil spirit which never deserts its post until death overtakes the beast and gives it notice to quit. We strain ourselves up, each in his own way, somewhat as Macready worked himself up for his great parts on the stage. "Mr. Macready, you know," said a director of Her Majesty's theatre, "when engaging his dresser, whom I knew very well, arranged that when he shook him he should pay him double wages, and when he struck him his pay should be trebled. I think that dresser used to get treble wages all the while Ma-

The Goojerat.

Macready.

cready was at Drury Lane. I went once to Macready's dressing-room during the performance. The tragedian had the dresser in the corner and was nearly choking him. He was rehearsing his part. He afterward rushed upon the stage and startled his audience by his brilliant acting." Talma, in order to work up his grand bursts of passion, would seize upon any unfortunate super whom he came upon behind the scenes, and shake him until he himself had become breathless and the man frightened beyond all control at his assumed violence. The peculiarities both of Macready and Talma were only in accordance with that precedent furnished in ancient history, though with less disastrous results. According to Plutarch, Æsop, the Roman actor, so interested himself in the characters he undertook that, one day, when he played Atreus, he in that scene where it falls to his lot to consider how he might best destroy the tyrant Thyestes, worked himself up into such a pitch of ungovernable rage that he struck one of the minor performers with his sceptre and laid him dead at his feet.

Marginalia: Rehearsing his part. Æsop, the Roman actor.

Human society is always swaying, backward and forward — vibrating, like the pendulum, from one extreme to another; for a moment only, now and then, is it upright, and governed by reason. Moderation is exceptional and hateful. Happy if the world's favorite to-day be not its victim to-morrow. A dramatist was walking one day in the Rue St. Honoré with his friend Talma, then at the commencement of his career, when a young officer in a shabby lieutenant's uniform met them, and said to the actor, "Remember to-morrow." Talma nodded assent, and the other passed on. "Who is that?" was asked. "The torment of my life," was the reply. "A young fellow without a sou, who is perpetually plaguing me for tickets of admission to the theatre. Not a bad judge, I must say," he continued. "Knows all our classics by heart, and won't listen to anything but Corneille and Racine." Some twenty years later, the two friends chanced to meet again in the Place du Carrousel, at the very moment when Napoleon was starting for his daily ride. On seeing Talma he stopped his horse, and spoke a few words to him. When he had left them, the tragedian, turning to his

Of Incalculable Forces.

Talma.

Napoleon.

companion, asked if he recollected the young lieutenant who used formerly to bother him for tickets. On the latter's confessing that he had quite forgotten the circumstance, "Ah," observed Talma, "I have more reason to remember him than you have. He is Emperor now, and I am a poor devil of an actor." The House of Commons impeached Warren Hastings in 1787; the House of Commons uncovered and stood up to receive him in 1813. Traveling through Switzerland, Napoleon was greeted with such enthusiasm that Bourrienne said to him, "It must be delightful to be greeted with such demonstrations of enthusiastic admiration." "Bah!" replied Napoleon, "this same unthinking crowd, under a slight change of circumstances, would follow me just as eagerly to the scaffold." Mirabeau, on a famous occasion, amid the threatening clamors of an angry crowd said, "A few days ago I too was to be carried in triumph, and now they are bawling through the streets, 'the great treason of the Count of Mirabeau.' This lesson was not necessary to remind me that the distance is short between the Capitol and the Tarpeian Rock." "What throngs! what acclamations," exclaimed the flatterers of Cromwell, when he was proclaimed Protector of the Commonwealth of England. Cromwell replied, "There would be still more, if they were going to hang me." The multitudes that went before and that followed Christ into Jerusalem, crying, "Hosanna to the Son of David: Blessed is he that cometh in the name of the Lord: Hosanna in the highest," "cried out again, Crucify him. Then Pilate said unto them, Why, what evil hath he done? and they cried out the more exceedingly, Crucify him." The elements of a riot are varied and mixed, like the composite clothes that were worn by Dennis, the hangman, in Barnaby Rudge — garments belonging to the persons he had hanged. Dickens, in his description of the Lord George Gordon riots, gives prominence, not only to Dennis, the executioner, but to Hugh, the brute, Simon Tappertitt, the locksmith's half-crazy apprentice, and Barnaby Rudge, the half-idiot. Every one remembers Hugo's analysis of a tumult. "Irritated convictions, embittered enthusiasms, aroused indignations, martial instincts suppressed, youthful courage exalted, and generous blindnesses; curiosity, a taste for a change,

The multitudes in Jerusalem.

Hugo's analysis.

thirst for something unexpected, the feeling which causes us to find pleasure in reading the announcement of a new piece, or on hearing the machinist's whistle; vague hatreds, rancors, disappointments, every vanity which believes that destiny has been a bankrupt to it; straitened circumstances, empty dreams, ambitions surrounded with escarpments, every man who hopes for an issue from an overthrow, and lastly, at the very bottom, the mob, that mud which takes fire — such are the elements of riot. The greatest and the most infamous, beings who prowl about beyond the pale of everything while awaiting an opportunity, gypsies, nameless men, highway vagabonds, the men who sleep o' nights in a desert of houses with no other roof but the cold clouds of heaven, those who daily ask their bread of chance, and not of toil; the unknown men of wretchedness and nothingness, with bare arms and bare feet, belong to the riot. Every man who has in his soul a secret revolt against any act of the state, of life, or of destiny, is on the border line of riot, and so soon as it appears, he begins to quiver and to feel himself lifted by the whirlwind."

"Few terrestrial appearances," says Carlyle, "are better worth considering than mobs. Your mob is a genuine outburst of nature, issuing from, or communicating with, the deepest deeps of nature. When so much goes grinning and grimacing as a lifeless formality, and under the stiff buckram no heart can be felt beating, here once more, if nowhere else, is a sincerity and reality. Shudder at it; or even shriek over it, if thou must; nevertheless consider it." "The world," said Goethe, "is not so framed that it can keep quiet; the great are not so that they will not permit misuse of power; the masses not so that, in hope of a gradual amelioration, they will keep tranquil in an inferior condition. Could we perfect human nature, we might expect perfection everywhere; but as it is, there will always be this wavering hither and thither; one part must suffer while the other is at ease." "It is with human things," says Froude, "as it is with the great icebergs which drift southward out of the frozen seas. They swim two thirds under water, and one third above; and so long as the equilibrium is sustained you would think that they were as stable as the rocks. But the sea water is warmer than the air. Hundreds of fathoms down, the

A genuine outburst of nature.

Shudder at it; consider it.

With human things as it is with icebergs.

tepid current washes the base of the berg. Silently, in those far deeps the centre of gravity is changed; and then, in a moment, with one vast roll, the enormous mass heaves over, and the crystal peaks which had been glancing so proudly in the sunlight are buried in the ocean forever." "The secret which you would fain keep, as soon as you go abroad, lo! there is one standing on the door-step to tell you the same." The revolution is all at once ripe, and the bottom is at the top again. Nobody and everybody is responsible. "It is seldom," says John Galt, in his life of Wolsey, "that any man can sway the current of national affairs; but a wide and earnest system of action never fails to produce results which resemble the preëxpected effects of particular designs." At the gorgeous coronation of Napoleon, some one asked the republican general Augereau whether anything was wanting to the splendor of the scene. "Nothing," replied Augereau, "but the presence of the million of men who have died to do away with all this."

The centre of gravity changed.

The bottom at the top again.

DECEIVING THROUGH THE AFFECTIONS.

The milking of the buffalo of the Campagna, outside of the city of Rome, is done

In a Club Corner

in the dark by a person who glides under the cow, covered with a buffalo skin. Carlyle, in his Cromwell, asks, "Did the reader ever see, or fancy in his mind, a tulchan? Tulchan is, or rather was, for the thing is long since obsolete, a calfskin stuffed into the rude similitude of a calf, — similar enough to deceive the imperfect perceptive organs of a cow. At milking-time the tulchan, with head duly bent, was set as if to suck; the fond cow looking round fancied that her calf was busy, and that all was right, and so gave her milk freely, which the cunning maid was straining in white abundance into her pail all the while." Deceiving through the affections has ever been in practice, and ever will be. Could the world speak as to effects of it, what lamentations we should hear.

Tulchan

There is a pretty legend of Jesus and two or three of his disciples going down, one summer day, from Jerusalem to Jericho. Peter — the ardent and eager Peter — was as usual by the Teacher's side. On the road on Olivet lay a horseshoe, which the Teacher desired Peter to pick up, but which Peter let lie, as he did not think it

A PRETTY LEGEND.

worth the trouble of stooping for. The Teacher stooped for it, and exchanged it in the village for a measure of cherries. These cherries he carried (as men there now carry such things) in the bosom folds of his dress. When they had to ascend the ridge, and the road lay between heated rocks, and over rugged stones and glaring white dust, Peter became tormented with heat and thirst, and fell behind. Then the Teacher dropped a ripe cherry at every few footsteps; and Peter eagerly stooped for them. When they were all gone, Jesus turned to him, and said with a smile, "He who is above stooping to a small thing, will have to bend his back to many lesser things."

The Teacher stooped.

It has been observed that "the bad memories are often the best, as they are almost sure to be the selecting memories. They seldom win distinction in examinations, except in literature and art. They are incomparably superior to the miscellaneous memories that receive only as boxes and drawers receive what is put into them. A good literary or artistic memory is not like a post-office that takes in everything, but like a very well edited periodical which

SELECTING MEMORIES.

prints nothing that does not harmonize with its intellectual life." Scott used to illustrate the capricious affinity of his own memory for what suited it, and its complete rejection of what did not, by old Beattie of Meikledale's answer to a Scotch divine who complimented him on the strength of his memory. "No, sir," said the old Borderer; "I have no command of my memory. It only retains what hits my fancy; and, probably, sir, if you were to preach to me for two hours, I would not be able, when you finished, to remember a word you had been saying." Henry Clay told Mrs. Mowatt, the actress, that he could not by any effort retain verse in his memory. Locke had no correct knowledge of fiction; and as to poetry he thought Blackmore as great a genius as Homer. Newton considered poetry as on a par with "ingenious nonsense"; but when the name of the Deity was mentioned, he took off his hat. "Buffon," said Madame de Staël, "knows not the world, but he knows the universe." Sydney Smith advised ignorance of a great number of things, in order to avoid the calamity of being ignorant of everything. "I remember," said Mr. Hookam Frere, "one day

Scott's illustration.

Newton's estimate of poetry.

going to consult Canning on a matter of great importance to me, when he was stopping at Enfield. We walked into the woods to have a quiet talk, and as we passed some ponds I was surprised to find that it was a new light to him that tadpoles turned into frogs. 'Now, don't you,' he added, 'go and tell that story to the next fool you meet.' Canning could rule, and did rule, a great and civilized nation, but people are apt to fancy that a man who does not know the natural history of frogs must be an imbecile in the treatment of men." Memory, to be of great value, it would appear, must be limited, ready, and at absolute command. A really valuable memory is impatient of diversion from accustomed employment, and when diverted, returns to it, naturally, and in the shortest manner. Leslie once found Coleridge driving the balls on a bagatelle board, for a kitten to run after them. He noticed that as soon as the little thing turned its back to the balls it seemed to forget all about them, and played with its tail — its favorite occupation. "I am amused," he said, "with the limits of their little memories." There is a terrible story in illustration of a confused memory, of a man

Marginal notes: Canning's ignorance as to tadpoles. / Coleridge amusing himself.

who made an abstruse conundrum and forgot the answer. After groping about his uncertain mind for several days, he gave it up in despair and cut his throat. De Quincey, though nothing of a Skimpole, in pecuniary matters, was, we are told, helpless beyond the traditional helplessness of literary characters — beyond even Goldsmith and Steele. Burton tells of his knocking a friend up late at night to raise a loan of a few shillings, offering to deposit as security a ten pound note which he had in his pocket, and which seems to have occurred to him rather as a negotiable instrument of some kind than as current money of the realm. This in spite of the fact that he wrote a work on political economy which Mill mentions with respect. There is an amusing story told of Lord Camden, when a barrister, having been fastened in stocks on top of a hill in order to gratify an idle curiosity on the subject. Being left there by the absent-minded friend who had locked him in, he found it impossible to procure his liberation for the greater part of the day. On his entreating a chance traveler to release him, the man shook his head and passed on, remarking that of course he was not there for nothing. There is a very curious incident of Beaumont and Fletcher, who were brought under suspicion of treason, because, while concerting the plan of a tragedy when sitting together at a tavern, one of them was overheard saying to the other, "I'll kill the king!" It is recorded of Peter Burrowes, the friend of Grattan, that, on circuit, a brother barrister found him at breakfast-time standing by the fire with an egg in his hand and his watch in the saucepan. La Fontaine, having attended the funeral of a friend, was so absent-minded as to call upon him a short time afterward. Being reminded of the fact, he was at first greatly surprised, but recollecting himself, said: "It is true enough, for I was there." When Coleridge, it is related, was a poor boy, and a charity scholar in London, he was one day walking along the Strand at an hour when the place was crowded, and was throwing out his arms vigorously toward the right and the left. One of his hands came into contact with a gentleman's waistcoat pocket, and the man immediately accused the boy of thieving intentions. "No," said Coleridge, "I am not intending to pick your pocket. I am swimming the Hellespont. This morning in school I read the story of Hero and Leander, and I am now imitating the latter as he swims from Asia to Europe." The gentleman was so much impressed by the vividness of the imagination of the lad that he subscribed for Coleridge's admission to a public library, which began the poet's education. It is very true, as said by a writer in an old number of the London Quarterly, that an interest attaches with every person of education to the name of Simson, from his admirable edition of the Elements of Euclid, a work which cost him nine years of labor. His long, tranquil, and amiable life appears to have been governed by the rigid rules of mathematics, which was the business and solace of his existence. He regulated his exercise by the number of paces, and after exchanging greetings with any acquaintance whom he met in his walks, he might be heard continuing the enumeration as he moved away. His absence of mind would have kept Ampère in countenance, and satisfied the skeptics of the reality of the propensity, though he differed from the Frenchman in being particularly methodical in his transaction of business. He was noted for his absent-mindedness. He used to sit at his open

Simson.

Methodical in business.

window on the ground floor, deep in geometry, and when accosted by a beggar would rouse himself, hear a few words of the story, make his donation, and dive again into his geometry. Some wags one day stopped a mendicant on his way to the window with — "Now, do as we tell you, and you will get something from that gentleman, and a shilling from us besides. He will ask who you are, and you will say, Robert Simson, son of John Simson of Kirktonhill." The man did as he was told; Simson gave him a coin and dropped off; but soon roused himself and said: "Robert Simson, son of John Simson of Kirktonhill! why, that is myself! That man must be an impostor!" The anecdotes which Lord Brougham has recovered of Adam Smith show that he too was liable to fits of abstraction which rendered him insensible to everything around him. At a dinner at Dalkeith he was animadverting upon the character of a statesman of the day, when observing his nearest relative at the table, he suddenly stopped. He speedily passed from open conversation into a fit of musing, and was heard muttering to himself, "De'il care, de'il care, it's all true." In walking through the streets

marginalia: A practical joke. / Adam Smith.

of Edinburgh, his hands behind him and his head in the air, he knocked against the passengers, and on one occasion overturned a stall, without the slightest consciousness of what he had done. "Heigh, sirs," said a female worthy in the Fishmarket, who took him for an absolute lunatic, "to let the like of him be about! And yet he's weel eneugh put on" (dressed). Ampère's solitary musings for many years of his life, we are told, had made abstraction habitual to him, and he naturally fell into it without regard to time or place. Hence he was extremely absent, and was guilty of a thousand unconscious eccentricities. He mistook the cloth for cleaning the blackboard, and which was always covered with chalk, for his pocket handkerchief. He carried away from a party the three-cornered chapeau of an ecclesiastic, and as the owner was a desirable acquaintance, it was asserted by the enemies of the philosopher that he designedly took the wrong hat (his own was a common round one) that he might have an excuse for calling next day to return it. Arago repudiates the paltry construction, and meets the imputation with a counter anecdote, in which Ampère's infirmity was not

Ampère's solitary musings.

Arago's counter anecdote.

calculated to recommend him. Invited to the table of a person whom it was of importance to conciliate, he suddenly exclaimed, "Really this dinner is detestable. My sister ought not to engage cooks without having personally satisfied herself of their capabilities." "Lord Dudley," said Sydney Smith, "was one of the most absent men I think I ever met in society. One day he met me in the street, and invited me to meet myself. 'Dine with me to-day; dine with me, and I will get Sydney Smith to meet you.' I admitted the temptation he held out to me, but said I was engaged to meet him elsewhere." Lessing, the German philosopher, being remarkably absent, knocked at his own door one evening, when the servant, looking out of an upper window and not recognizing him, said, "The professor is not at home." "Oh, very well," replied Lessing, composedly walking away; "I shall call another time." Dr. Campbell, the author of The Survey of Great Britain, was so absent-minded that, looking into a pamphlet at a bookseller's, he liked it so well that he purchased it, and it was not until he had read it half through that he discovered it to be his own composition. On a trial for murder, it was important to the prisoner that the bullet found in the wound should be produced. It was handed to Burrowes, who was occasionally taking a lozenge for hoarseness. In the middle of his speech he paused, and suddenly exclaimed, "Oh Lord, I have swallowed the bullet!" Plunket said of him: "He has spent his life in doing acts of kindness to every human being but himself. He has been prodigal of his time, of his trouble, of his talents, of his money, to every human being who had or had not a claim, and this to the serious neglect of his own interests. In short, I can only account for such an anomaly as this, by supposing him utterly destitute of the instinct of selfishness." Barry Cornwall relates that George Dyer invited some one — he thinks it was Llanos, the author of Esteban and Sandoval — to breakfast with him one day in Clifford's Inn. Dyer of course forgot all about the matter very speedily after giving the invitation; and when Llanos went at the appointed hour, he found nothing but little Dyer, and his books and his dust — the work of years — at home. George, however, was anything but inhospitable, as far as his means or ideas went; and on

Swallowed the bullet.

George Dyer.

being told that Llanos had come to breakfast, proceeded to investigate his cupboard. He found the remnant of a threepenny loaf, two cups and saucers, a little glazed teapot, and a spoonful of milk. They sat down, and (Dyer putting the hot water into the teapot) commenced breakfast. Llanos attacked the stale crust, and waited with much good humor and patience for his tea. At last, out it came. Dyer, who was half blind, kept pouring out — nothing but hot water from the teapot, until Llanos, who thought a man might be guilty of too much abstinence, inquired if D. had not forgot the tea. "God bless me!" replied D., "and so I have." He began immediately to remedy his error, and emptied the contents of a piece of brown paper into the teapot, deluged it with water, and sat down with a look of complete satisfaction. "How very odd it was that I should make such a mistake!" said Dyer. However, he now determined to make amends, and filled Llanos' cup again. Llanos thought the tea had a strange odor, but not having dread of aqua tofana before his eyes, he thrust his spoon in and tasted. It was ginger! Seeing that it was in vain to expect common-

At breakfast.

Forgot the tea.

It was ginger!

places from the little absentee, Llanos continued cutting and crumbling a little bread into his plate for a short time and then departed. He went straight to a coffee-house in the neighborhood, and was just finishing a capital breakfast when Dyer came in, to read the paper, or to inquire after some one who frequented the coffee-house. He recognized Llanos, and asked how he did; but felt no surprise at seeing him devouring a second breakfast. He had totally forgotten all the occurrences of the morning. Crabb Robinson wrote in his Diary: "After going to University College Committee, I went to J. Taylor's to exchange hats, having taken his last night; but he had not mine there. I took an omnibus to Addison Road, drank tea with Paynter, and then went to Taylor's to restore his hat; and then I found that I had a second time blundered by bringing Paynter's old hat; and I lost an hour in going to and from Addison Road, and from and to Sheffield House. Is this infirmity incurable? I fear it is; though I record it here to assist me in becoming more on my guard. It is a wise saying of Horace Walpole's, 'There is no use in warning a man of his folly, if you do not cure him of being foolish.'" One of Emerson's friends relates a little incident of his late years, illustrating his forgetfulness and simplicity. His daughter used to collect and keep the leaves of his lecture manuscripts, putting them in his hands before he began, and taking care of them when he had done. On one occasion he was lecturing in Boston, when suddenly, in the midst of an interesting branch of his theme, he sat down. Supposing he did so to rest, the people waited: but soon they saw he had no more to say, and withdrew. Afterward some one said to him, that he had closed rather abruptly. "It seemed so to me," he replied, "but that was all that Ellen gave me!" Garrick's third master, according to Fitzgerald, was a Mr. Colson, a clergyman, and a dreamy scholar, very absent, and almost totally indifferent to his family concerns, from delight in his scientific studies. This philosopher lived entirely in an upper room of his house, where none of his family dared intrude. When he came down, he seemed to be walking about like a total stranger. Not without humor, and most probably founded in truth, is the description of two instances of utter indifference to the mere social events of the world that

Emerson's forgetfulness.

Garrick's third master.

were unconnected with science. He receives a letter, and having given it to his servant to read, it was found to bring news of his brother's shipwreck, and of his being left naked and destitute in a foreign country. "Naked and destitute!" exclaimed he abstractedly; "reach me down the last volume of meteorological observations!" When they came to tell him of a fire that was advancing so rapidly on all sides that the inhabitants were only thinking of their lives, he said with interest, "What you tell me is very probable, for fire naturally moves in a circle." Such a character, it is remarked, would have been a subject for the gay mimicry of his pupil, who may have described it to his friend Dr. Johnson: it certainly answers to the delineation (Gelidus) in the Rambler, No. 24. The distinguished Lessing, before referred to — sometimes called the Luther of German Literature — having missed money at different times without being able to discover who took it, determined to put the honesty of his servant to the test, and left a handful of gold on the table. "Of course you counted it," said one of his friends. "Counted it!" said Lessing, rather embarrassed, — "no; I forgot that." A story

News of his brother's shipwreck.

Gelidus, in the Rambler.

Chief Justice Marshall. is told of Chief Justice Marshall, that, on returning once from North Carolina, intent on some knotty point of law, he found himself suddenly brought to a halt by a small tree. Seeing a servant near by, he asked him to bring an axe and cut down the tree. The servant told the judge that there was no necessity for cutting down the sapling, but just to back his buggy. Pleased at the good sense of the fellow, he told him that he would leave him something at the inn hard by, where he intended stopping, having then no small change. In due time the servant applied, and a dollar was handed him. Being asked if he knew who it was that gave him the money, he replied, "No, sir; I knew he was a gentleman by his leaving the dollar, but I think he is the biggest fool I ever saw."

MANNERS. "When I arrived at Buckingham House," says Mrs. Siddons, in her autobiographical Memoranda, "I was conducted into an antechamber, where I found some ladies of my acquaintance; and, in a short time, the king entered from the drawing-room, in the amiable occupation of drawing the princess Amelia, then scarce three years old, in a little cane-chair. He graciously

In a Club Corner

said something to one of the ladies, and left the lovely baby to run about the room. She happened to be much pleased with some flowers in my bosom, and, as I stooped down that she might take them, if so disposed, I could not help exclaiming to a lady near me, 'What a beautiful child!— how I long to kiss her!' when she instantly held her little hand to my mouth to be kissed: so early had she learned this lesson of royalty." The easy way of Archbishop Whately has been described: "He was of a gigantic size and a gaunt aspect, with a strange unconsciousness of the body; and what is perhaps the next best thing to manner, he had no manner. What his legs and arms were about was best known to themselves. His rank placed him by the side of the lord lieutenant's wife when dining at the castle, and the wife of one of the lord lieutenants has said that she had occasionally to remove the archbishop's foot out of her lap." There is the terrible gift of familiarity, as Pope Gregory called it, which the Marquis of Mirabeau applied to his son the Count. "He turns the great people here round his finger." Says Carlyle: "He has opened his far-sounding voice, the depths of his

Archbishop Whately.

The terrible gift of familiarity.

far-sounding soul; he can quell (such virtue is in a spoken word) the pride-tumults of the rich, the hunger-tumults of the poor; and wild multitudes move under him, as under the moon do billows of the sea; he has become a world-compeller, and ruler over men." Prince Bismarck, when he went into Paris with the troops, was recognized by the people, but no demonstration against him followed. There was one man, however, who scowled at him in a very noticeable manner. The prince at once rode up to him and begged a light for his cigar, and the ugly scowl instantly disappeared. At the beginning of the Revolutionary War, a large party of Virginia riflemen, who had recently arrived in camp, were strolling about Cambridge, and viewing the collegiate buildings, now turned into barracks. Their half-Indian equipments, and fringed and ruffled hunting garbs, provoked the merriment of some troops from Marblehead, chiefly fishermen and sailors, who thought nothing equal to the round jacket and trowsers. A bantering ensued between them. There was snow upon the ground, and snowballs began to fly when jokes were wanting. The parties waxed warm with the contest. They

Prince Bismarck.

An incident of the Revolutionary War.

closed, and came to blows; both sides were reinforced, and in a little while at least a thousand were at fisticuffs, and there was a tumult in the camp worthy of the days of Homer. "At this juncture," wrote an informant, "Washington made his appearance, whether by accident or design, I never knew. I saw none of his aides with him; his black servant was just behind him mounted. He threw the bridle of his horse into his servant's hands, sprang from his seat, rushed into the thickest of the mêlée, seized two tall brawny riflemen by the throat, keeping them at arm's length, talking to and shaking them. His appearance and strong-handed rebuke put an instant end to the tumult. The combatants dispersed in all directions, and in less than three minutes more there remained on the ground but the two he had collared." "Self-respect," in the judgment of Emerson, "is the early form in which greatness appears. You say of some new person, That man will go far,— for you see in his manners that the recognition of him by others is not necessary to him. And what a bitter-sweet sensation when we have gone to pour out our acknowledgment of a man's nobleness, and found him quite indifferent to

Washington made his appearance.

The early form in which greatness appears.

our good opinion." "Too much, I have perceived," remarks De Quincey, "in men that pass for good men, a disposition to degrade (and if possible to degrade through self-degradation) those in whom unwillingly they feel any weight of oppression to themselves, by commanding qualities of intellect or character. They respect you: they are compelled to do so, and they hate to do so." They lie in wait to humiliate or overpower you, — encouraged by occasional successful instances of combined weakness over individual strength, as in the famous triumph of the Lilliputians over Gulliver. "Do you think to distinguish yourself with impunity?" said Northcote to Hazlitt. "Do you imagine that your superiority will be delightful to others, or that they will not strive all that they can, and to the last moment, to pull you down? I remember myself once saying to Opie, how hard it was upon the poor author or player to be hunted down for not succeeding in an innocent and laudable attempt, just as if they had committed some heinous crime; and he answered, 'They have committed the greatest crime in the eyes of mankind — that of pretending to a superiority over them.'"

Artists are fond of painting their own portraits. In Florence there is a gallery of hundreds of them, including the most illustrious, in all of which there are, as Hawthorne remarks, autobiographical characteristics, so to speak; traits, expressions, loftinesses, and amenities, which would have been invisible had they not been painted from within. Yet their reality and truth are none the less. There is no more remarkable bit of self-portraiture than that by Saint Évremond: "He is a philosopher who keeps aloof alike from superstition and from impiety; an epicurean, whose distaste for debauchery is as strong as his appetite for pleasure; a man who has never known want, but at the same time has never enjoyed affluence. He lives in a manner which is despised by those who have everything, envied by those who have nothing, appreciated by those who make their happiness and their reason agree. In his youth he hated waste, being persuaded that property was necessary to make a long life comfortable. In his age he cares not for economy, feeling that want is little to be feared when one has but a little time to want in. He is grateful for the gifts of nature, and finds no fault with those of fortune; he hates crime, endures error, and pities misfortune. He does not try to find out the bad points of men in order to decry them, but he looks for their foibles in order to give himself amusement; is secretly rejoiced at the knowledge of these foibles, and would be still more pleased to make them known to others, did not his discretion forbid. Life is to his mind too short to read all sorts of books, and to load one's memory with all sorts of things at the risk of one's judgment. He devotes himself not to the most learned writings, so as to acquire knowledge, but to the most sensible, so as to strengthen his understanding. At one time he seeks the most elegant to refine his taste, at another the most amusing to refresh his spirits. As for friendship, he has more constancy than might be expected from a philosopher, and more heartiness than could be looked for even in a younger and less experienced man. As for religion, he thinks justice, charity, and trust in the goodness of God of more importance than sorrow for past offenses."

Life too short to read all sorts of books.

THE PHI-
LOSOPHER'S
STONE.

Douglas Jerrold expresses the opinion that the true philosopher's stone is only intense impudence. Perhaps, — we should say, — but with a generous tempering of self-possession and readiness. So qualified and fortified, to the common eye, it has the look of omnipotence. At the point of sublimity it dazzles, and is superhuman to the multitude. Only intelligence can penetrate it, and know its true character. One night at the theatre of San Carlo, Naples, Dumas the elder found himself chatting familiarly with a stranger who, when the play was over, said to him patronizingly: "I have greatly enjoyed your conversation, sir, and hope to see more of you. If ever you visit Paris call on me, I am Alexandre Dumas." "The devil you are! So am I!" replied the novelist, with a burst of laughter. Such impudent audacity, with a due admixture of self-possession and facility, seldom fails of its purpose. "Behold me now," says Rousseau, in his Confessions, "a teacher of singing, without knowing how to decipher an air. Without the least knowledge of composition, I boasted of my skill in it before all the world; and without ability to score the slenderest vaudeville, I gave myself out for a composer. Having been presented to M. de Treytorens, a professor of law, who loved music

The look of omnipotence.

Rousseau.

and gave concerts at his house, I insisted on giving him a specimen of my talent, and I set to work to compose a piece for his concert with as much effrontery as if I knew all about it." The performance came off duly, and the strange impostor conducted it with as much gravity as the profoundest master. Never since the beginning of opera had the like charivari greeted the ears of men. A friend of John Law asked him one day, whether it was true that he was going to war with England. "I should think," added he, "that a minister like yourself, whose interest it is to make the State flourish by commerce, and by establishments that require peace, would never think of going to war." Law replied, with the utmost calmness, "I do not desire war, but am not afraid of it." Frederic the Great once saw a crowd staring at something on a wall. He rode up, and found that the object of curiosity was a scurrilous placard against himself. The placard had been posted up so high that it was not easy to read it. Frederic ordered his attendants to take it down and put it lower. "My people and I," he said, "have come to an agreement which satisfies us both. They are to say what they please, and I am to do what I please." At the time of the Gordon riots, in June, 1780, Grimaldi resided in a front room on the second floor in Holborn, on the same side of the way near to Red Lion Square, when the mob passing by the house, and Grimaldi being a foreigner, they thought he must be a Papist. On hearing he lived there, they all stopped, and there was a general shouting; a cry of "No Popery" was raised, and they were about to assail the house, when Grimaldi put his head out of the window from the second floor, and, making comical grimaces, called out, "Gentlemen, in dis house dare be no religion at all." Laughing at their mistake, the mob proceeded on, first giving him three huzzas, though his house, unlike all the others, had not written on the door, "No Popery." A marauder, arrested for a highway robbery, on being brought before a magistrate, asserted that he was more entitled to be pitied than to be punished. "Pitied!" exclaimed the justice, whilst his eyebrows arched with more than ordinary wonder and contempt; "and on what account, pray?" "Sure on account of my misfortune." "Your misfortune, indeed! What, that we have caught you, I sup-

Grimaldi.

A marauder to be pitied.

The culprit's misfortune.

pose?" "Oh, the jintleman that's brought me here knows my misfortune well enough." But the gentleman was as astonished as the magistrate himself, and as incapable of guessing the culprit's meaning. "You will own, I suppose," said his worship, "that you stopped this gentleman on the highway?" "Oh, yes. I did that same." "And that you took from him fifty pounds in Bank of Wexford bills?" "And there your honor's right again." "Well, then, you perplexing vagabond, what do you mean by your misfortune?" "Sure, I mean that the money was n't in my pocket above a week, when the dirty bank stopped payment, and I was robbed of every shillin'!"

READING ALOUD.

Draper, I think, somewhere in his History of the Intellectual Development of Europe, observes, that if there are disadvantages in the method of acquiring knowledge by reading, there are also signal advantages; for, though upon the printed page the silent letters are mute and unsustained by any scenic help, yet often — a wonderful contradiction — they pour forth emphatic eloquence, that can make the heart leap with emotion, or kindle on the cheek the blush of shame. The might of persuasiveness does not always lie in articulate speech. The strong are of the silent. God never speaks. We are as elastic, says Emerson, as the gas of gunpowder, and a sentence in a book sets free our fancy, and instantly our heads are bathed with galaxies, and our feet tread the floor of the Pit. Yet on the other hand there are readers so careless, so indifferent, so insensate, as to appear to be proof against emotion — to say nothing of intellectual exaltation. Don Abbondio, the cowardly priest in Manzoni's story, may be cited as an instance; he was very fond of reading a little every day; and a neighboring curate, who possessed something of a library, lent him one book after another, always taking the first that came to hand. All printed matter was alike to him.

The strong are of the silent.

Reading aloud, as a mere physical exercise, is of great importance and efficacy. Cicero, in some one of his letters, speaks of curing himself of troublesome and alarming weakness by reading aloud for some hours every day. Certain temperaments are influenced by it as actors are affected by their own playing. It is said of Madame Pasta that she would come home from the opera, and sit in a passion of tears at the

Reading aloud as a physical exercise.

recollection of what she had been acting. It was entirely unaffected. She would say she knew it to be idle, but that she " could not get the thing out of her head."

Cross, in his Life of George Eliot, expresses the belief that reading requires for its perfection a rare union of intellectual, moral, and physical qualities. It cannot be imitated. It is an art, like singing — a personal possession that dies with the possessor, and leaves nothing behind except a memory. Immediately before his wife's last illness, they read together the first part of Faust. Reading the poem in the original with such an interpreter was the opening of a new world to him. Nothing in all literature moved her more, he tells us, than the pathetic situation and the whole character of Gretchen. It touched her more than anything in Shakespeare.

George Eliot's reading.

In one of Sir Henry Taylor's published letters he speaks of reading Shakespeare to his children, and adds: " Reading of Shakespeare to boys and girls (if it be well read, and if they be apt), I regard as carrying with it a deeper cultivation than anything else that can be done to cultivate them; and I often think how strange it is that amongst all the efforts which are made in these times to teach young people everything that is to be known, from the cedar of Lebanon to the hyssop on the wall, the one thing omitted is teaching them to read."

In the book of Nehemiah is given, in a few words, the true standard of reading — *The true standard of reading.* how Ezra, the learned and pious priest, and the Levites, read to the people the law of Moses: "They read in the book, in the law of God, distinctly, and gave the sense, and caused the people to understand the reading." They "gave the sense," be it observed, and the people understood it. The Persian poet Saadi tells that a person with a disagreeable voice was reading the Koran aloud, when a holy man, passing by, asked what was his monthly stipend. He answered, "Nothing at all." "But why then do you take so much trouble?" He replied, "I read for the sake of God." The other rejoined, "For God's sake do not read; for if you read the Koran in this manner you will destroy the splendor of *The splendor of Islamism in danger.* Islamism."

How strange, that of the multitudes of readers, so few comparatively should be able to read aloud agreeably and intelligibly. Is reading aloud such a difficult art? or is all the world indifferent about acquiring it? It cannot be that of the many branches of education, the most important should be the most neglected. A thing so preposterous is incredible. There must be causes inscrutable to account for a fact so extraordinary. Considering the pleasure to others derived from agreeable and intelligible oral reading, to say nothing of its economy, one would think that, of all things, it would be most anxiously studied and most diligently practiced. Can it be indeed that good readers are born, and not made? Can it be that the infinite many are wanting in the faculties and qualities necessary to attain the art? Would some one could tell the essentialities so rare! The best vocal readers, we know, are not always the best intellects. Apparently, they only possess a certain ken, which is characteristic, but undefinable. They perceptibly penetrate the words, perceive the sense, and participate the feeling, which they are able unconsciously to interpret, reveal, and enkindle in the reading. If you undertake to analyze the achievement — to talk of manner, voice, pronunciation, intonation, inflection, or anything incident to it — you are in a

Causes inscrutable.

The essentialities so rare.

labyrinth without a clue. There is not anything, you may say, which is more simple and at the same time more inexplicable than good oral reading. The author of the composition, being present at the reading of it by a good reader, is more astonished than any other hearer. Beauty, or strength, or feeling, is revealed to him he had not dreamed of. An apple falls, on its way to the centre of the earth: a good reader penetrates intuitively the marrow of the printed page, and plucks its substance and flavor. A name is given by philosophy to the former — gravitation; but there is no word in the language for the latter. An excellence so superior and so exceptional as reading aloud agreeably, intelligibly, and impressively, one would think, should have a name to distinguish it from ordinary reading, as oratory is distinguished from ordinary speaking. The rules and laws and machinery of what is called elocution have little or nothing to do with good reading but to make it impossible. I once went in upon a class in elocution, and found the teacher soberly instructing his pupils by the use of the blackboard — lines being drawn thereon, and notes written within, as in music — the

Beauty, etc., not dreamed of.

A ludicrous scene.

words to be pitched and accented and intoned accordingly! The worst effect of all the bad effects of professional elocution is to create and foster excessive self-consciousness — a condition wholly inconsistent with intelligent and satisfactory reading, if not absolutely inimical to it. Go into a school-room, filled with big pupils. Say to the teacher interrogatively that you hope he has some good readers, and he does not understand you. Go into the churches, and hear how the Scriptures, as a rule, are read. I do not remember to have heard the Bible perfectly read but once, and that was by an African bishop, not distinguished for his erudition. Even the child with me was interested in the reading — she understood it.

Self-consciousness inimical.

"In company with a friend to whom Garrick had promised some instructions in the character of Macbeth, I waited on him (says Cooke) at his house in the Adelphi about eleven o'clock on a Sunday morning. After some preliminary conversation, Garrick took up the play, and read several passages with a taste, feeling, and discrimination, new even to me, who had seen him so often in this character on the stage. But when he came to the dagger scene, I ob-

Garrick's reading.

served his face instantly assume a mixture of horror, perplexity, and guilt, which I thought it impossible for human nature to affect: the glare of his eye was conformable to the range of his features, and he went through the passage in a style totally indescribable. I then saw the amazing effect of his art; in which, like a great original in painting, the nearer it was viewed, the more the delicate and master touches of the pencil were discernible. The event happened about thirty years ago; and I now remember it with a sensibility which, while it affords me the most lively impressions, leads me to despair of ever 'seeing its like again.'"

Its amasing effect.

In his Memoirs, he also makes reference to Dr. Johnson's remarkable reading. The doctor read serious and sublime poetry with very great gravity and feeling. In the recital of prayers and religious poems he was awfully impressive, and his memory served him upon these occasions with great readiness. One night at the club a person quoting the nineteenth psalm, the doctor caught fire; and, instantly taking off his hat, began with great solemnity, —

Johnson's remarkable reading.

"The spacious firmament on high," etc., —

and went through that beautiful hymn.

Those who were acquainted with the doctor, knew how harsh and repulsive his features in general were; but on this occasion, to use the language of Scripture, "his face was almost as if it had been the face of an angel."

THE OB-LIQUE TENDENCY.

It was the opinion of Lord Lytton — expressed in his little story of Money — that the vices and the virtues are written in a language the world cannot construe — it reads them in a vile translation, and the translators are Failure and Success. Carlyle was very angry with Emerson for not believing in a devil, and to convert him took him amongst all the horrors of London — the gin-shops, etc. — and finally to the House of Commons, plying him at every turn with the question, "Do you believe in a devil noo?" A young tragedienne could not satisfy Voltaire in a passage in one of his tragedies, and he gave the passage himself as he thought it ought to be delivered. "Why," said she, "I should have to have the devil in me to reach the tone you wish!" "Exactly so, mademoiselle!" cried the author. "It is the devil you must have in you, to excel in any of the arts." Crébillon wrote effective trag-

Voltaire and the young tragedienne.

edies, chiefly remarkable for their power to excite terror. Being questioned, after the successful production of one of his terrific plays, as to his reason for choosing that line, he answered, "Corneille has appropriated heaven, and Racine the earth. Nothing remained for me but the domain of his Satanic majesty, and I threw myself into it headlong." Washington Irving, in his journal of a trip to Montreal in 1808, speaks of an Irish fellow-passenger, who took a fancy to him and his party, and was a great resource to them in the tedium of the passage, by his stories of fun and frolic. In Montreal the jolly fellow called to beg them not to whisper a word of his capers on the journey, "for I'm a praist, you see, and in this country a praist is the devil." There is a curious legend, current in the neighborhood of Moscow, that when the devil once tried to creep into Paradise, he took the form of a mouse; the dog and cat were on guard at the gates, and the dog allowed the evil one to pass, but the cat pounced on him, and so defeated another treacherous attempt against human felicity. To those who would kill him outright, a lesson of interest and of profit may be found in Rabelais. "Gymnast asked Gar-

Crébillon's reason for his choice.

As to killing the devil.

gantua if they should pursue the enemy? To whom Gargantua answered, By no means; for according to right military discipline, you must never drive your enemy into despair, for that such a strait doth multiply his force, and increase his courage, which was before broken and cast down; neither is there any better help, or outgate of relief for men that are amazed, out of heart, toiled, and spent, than to hope for no favor at all. How many victories have been taken out of the hands of the victors by the vanquished, when they would not rest satisfied with reason, but attempt to put all to the sword, and totally to destroy their enemies, without leaving so many as one to carry home news of the defeat of his fellows. Open, therefore, unto your enemies all the gates and ways, and make to them a bridge of silver rather than fail, that you may be rid of them." Goethe's conception of the character and reasoning of Mephistopheles, the tempting spirit in the play of Faust, appeared to Scott, in Quentin Durward, more happy than that which has been formed by Byron, and even by the Satan of Milton. "These last great authors have given to the Evil Principle something which elevates and dignifies his

Never drive your enemy into despair.

The Satan of Milton.

wickedness; a sustained and unconquerable resistance against Omnipotence itself — a lofty scorn of suffering compared with submission, and all those points of attraction in the Author of Evil, which have induced Burns and others to consider him as the Hero of the Paradise Lost. The great German poet has, on the contrary, rendered his seducing spirit a being who, otherwise totally unimpassioned, seems only to have existed for the purpose of increasing, by his persuasions and temptations, the mass of moral evil, and who calls forth by his seductions those slumbering passions which otherwise might have allowed the human being who was the object of the Evil Spirit's operations to pass the tenor of his life in tranquillity. For this purpose Mephistopheles is, like Louis XI., endowed with an acute and depreciating spirit of caustic wit which is employed incessantly in undervaluing and vilifying all actions, the consequences of which do not lead certainly and directly to self-gratification." Miss Martineau says of her early life: "I did not at any time, I think, believe in the devil, but understood the Scriptures to speak of sin under that name, and of eternal detriment under the name of eternal

Mephistopheles.

Like Louis XI.

punishment. I believed in inestimable and eternal rewards of holiness; but I am confident that I never in my life did a right thing or abstained from a wrong one from any consideration of reward or punishment."

WHISTLING. A writer in The Gentleman's Magazine, on the authority of Captain Burton, tells us how the Arabs dislike whistling. Some maintain that the whistler's mouth is not to be purified for forty days, while, according to the explanation of others, Satan touching a man's body causes him to produce what they consider an offensive sound. The natives of the Tonga Islands, Polynesia, hold it to be wrong to whistle, as this act is thought to be disrespectful to God. In Iceland the villagers have the same objection to whistling, and so far do they carry their superstitious dread of it that "if one swings about him a stick, whip, wand, or aught that makes a whistling sound, he scares from him the Holy Ghost," while other Icelanders who consider themselves free from superstitions *Do it not.* cautiously give the advice: "Do it not; for who knoweth what is in the air?" A correspondent of Notes and Queries relates how one day, after attempting in vain to get his dog to obey orders to come into the house, his wife tried to coax it by whistling, when she was suddenly interrupted by a servant, a Roman Catholic, who exclaimed in the most piteous accents, "If you please, ma'am, don't whistle — every time a woman whistles the heart of the blessed Virgin bleeds." In some districts of North Germany the villagers say that if one whistles in the evening it makes the angels weep. It is a widespread superstition that it is at all times unlucky for women to whistle, which, according to one legend, originated in the circumstance that while the nails for our Lord's cross were being forged, a woman stood by and whistled. "Do it not; for who knoweth what is in the air?" *The heart of the Virgin bleeds.*

Morley tells us that when Rousseau and his music-teacher were in Lyons together, the latter fell into an epileptic fit in the street. Rousseau called for help, informed the crowd of the poor man's hotel, and then seizing a moment when no one was thinking about him, turned the street corner, and finally disappeared, the musician being thus abandoned by the only friend *Sentimentalism.*

on whom he had a right to count. It thus appears that a man may be exquisitely moved by the sound of bells, the song of birds, the fairness of smiling gardens, and yet be capable all the time, without a qualm of misgiving, of leaving a friend senseless in the road in a strange place. Barry Cornwall states that some years ago Mr. Charles Kemble on entering Brussels found that there was preparation making for an execution that occupied a good deal of attention. Three men were to be executed; but one man was remarkable for having committed almost twenty assassinations — having broken prison, etc., and for being a person of remarkable talent. Mr. Kemble determined to witness the spectacle. Now it is to be remembered that at Brussels they do not (or did not) execute any criminals after a certain hour in the day; and in order not to run too near this hour, the culprits are taken to the block some considerable time beforehand. The two undistinguished rogues were melancholy enough; but the notorious one was anything but chap fallen. He was well-dressed, had a good carriage, hummed a popular air, and in all other things exhibited the extreme of self-possession. On his way to the

Preparing for an execution.

The notorious rogue.

guillotine (or when he arrived there) he said, "Now don't mix my head with those fellows'; keep it apart. I would not have it supposed that I had such a rascally look as either of these vagabonds for the world." The Maréchale de Luxembourg was the oracle of fashion, and her decisions on everything in high life were without appeal. "One Sunday morning (says Madame de Genlis) we waited only for the Prince of Conti's arrival to celebrate mass; we were all seated round a table in the drawing-room, on which lay our prayer-books, which the maréchale amused herself by turning over. All at once she stopped at two or three prayers, which seemed to her to be in the worst possible taste, and of which, in fact, the expressions were somewhat singular. She made some very bitter remarks on these prayers; upon which I suggested to her, that it was enough if they were repeated with sincere piety, and that God certainly paid no attention to what we call good or bad taste. 'Oh Madame,' cried the maréchale very gravely, 'don't take such a notion as that into your head!'" Barham tells of an old woman on board a vessel who told some of her friends that, while she was at Margate

Heads not to be mixed.

A question of taste.

in the course of the summer, the friend at whose house she had been staying had gone into the market for the purpose of purchasing a goose. There were but two in the whole place offered for sale, by a girl of fourteen, who refused to part with one without the other, assigning no other reason for her obstinacy than that it was her mother's order. Not wishing for two geese, the lady at first declined to purchase, but at last finding there was no other to be had, and recollecting that a neighbor might be prevailed upon to take one off her hands, she concluded the bargain. Having paid for and secured the pair, she asked the girl at parting if she knew her mother's reason for the directions she had given. "Oh, yes, mistress," answered the young poultry-merchant readily, "mother said that they had lived together for eleven years, and it would be a sin and a shame to part them now." Mlle. Flachsland, who married Herder, writes to her betrothed that one night in the depth of the woods, she fell on her knees as she looked at the moon, and that having found some glow-worms she put them into her hair, being careful to arrange them in couples that she might not disturb their loves!

Not to be parted.

Glow-worms in couples.

"Nothing," in the judgment of Sir Joshua Reynolds, "is denied to well-directed labor; nothing is to be attained without it." "Excellence in any department," said Johnson, "can be attained only by the labor of a lifetime; it is not to be purchased at a lesser price." Carlyle wrote to a literary aspirant: "My dear young friend, you must learn the indispensable significance of hard, stern, long-continued labor. Grudge not labor, grudge not pain, disappointment, sorrow, or distress of any kind — all is for your good, if you can endeavor and endure. If you cannot, why then all is hopeless. No man ever grew to anything who durst not look death itself in the face, and say to all kinds of martyrdom, 'Ye shall not subdue me!' Be of courage; a man lies in you; but a man is not born the second time, any more than the first, without travail." Lamb related that when at Oxford he saw Milton's MS. of L'Allegro, etc., and was grieved to find from the corrections and erasures how the poet had labored upon them. He had fancied that they had come from his mind almost spontaneously. He said that to be a true poet a man must serve a long and rigorous apprenticeship. He must, like the mathematician, sit with a wet towel about his head if he wished to excel. Godwin wrote his Caleb Williams backwards — beginning, that is to say, with the last chapter, and working on to the first. Richardson produced his novels by painfully elaborating different portions at different times. Burton, Butler, Locke, Fuller, Warburton, and many others, laboriously kept commonplace books. Before Addison commenced his Spectator he had amassed three folio volumes of materials. Sheridan and Hook, it is well known, were always on the alert for brilliant bits of conversation and stray jokes, which they took good care to jot down in their pocket-books for future use. Pope, we are informed, scribbled down stray thoughts whenever they struck him — at a dinner-table, in an open carriage, at his toilet, and in bed. Hogarth would sketch on his finger-nail any face that struck him, hence the marvelous diversity of feature in his infinite galleries of portraits. Swift would lie in bed in the morning, "thinking of wit for the day," as Hook made up his impromptus the night before. Washington Irving was fond of taking his portfolio out into the fields, and laboriously manipulating his graceful periods while swinging on a stile. Lord Truro, like Demosthenes, had an impediment in his speech, but he overcame it by forming a list of synonyms, which he substituted for the words he could not pronounce. "Every bon mot that I utter," said Goethe, "costs me a purseful of money; half a million of my private fortune has passed through my hands that I might learn what I know now; — not only the whole of my father's fortune, but my salary, and my large literary income for more than fifty years." To Helvetius, a young writer, Voltaire wrote: "It costs you nothing to think, but it costs infinitely to write. I therefore preach to you eternally that art of writing which Boileau has so well known and so well taught: that respect for the language, that connection and sequence of ideas, that air of ease with which he conducts his readers, that naturalness which is the fruit of art, and that appearance of facility which is due to toil alone. A word out of place spoils the most beautiful thought." Boileau counseled writers to remand their works twenty times to the anvil, and he advised Racine to compose laboriously easy verses. Garrick told Henderson he was

Overcoming an impediment.

Voltaire to Helvetius.

Boileau's advice.

two months rehearsing Benedict before he could satisfy himself that he had modeled his action and recital to his idea of the part. Wordsworth said that sometimes whole weeks were employed in shaping two or three lines, before he could satisfy himself with their structure. Thomson was fourteen or fifteen years writing the Castle of Indolence. It is told of Lincoln's boyhood that of the books he did not own he took voluminous notes, filling his copy-book with choice extracts, and poring over them until they were fixed in his memory. He could not afford to waste paper upon his own original compositions. He would sit by the fire at night and cover the wooden shovel with essays and arithmetical exercises, which he would shave off, and begin again. Agassiz began his studies in natural history by copying hundreds of pages from a Lamarck which some one had lent him. Madame de Genlis said to Moore that she had lost thirty or forty volumes of extracts which she had made during a most voluminous course of English reading. She deposited them for safe-keeping, and never recovered them. Richter, before his seventeenth year, had made many thick volumes, each of them of more than three hundred quarto pages. One reason for it, he read books that were not always his own. Bentley is said by *Bentley.* Monk, his biographer, to have practiced throughout life the precaution of noting in the margins of his books the suggestions and conjectures which rushed into his mind during their perusal. To this habit of laying up materials in store may be partly attributed the surprising rapidity with which some of his most important works were completed. Irving relates that he was once riding with Moore in Paris, *Anecdote of Moore.* when the hackney-coach went suddenly into a rut, out of which it came with such a jolt as to send their heads bumping against the roof. "By Jove, I've got it!" cried Moore, clapping his hands with great glee. "Got what?" said Irving. "Why," said the poet, "that word which I have been hunting for six weeks to complete my last song. That beneficent driver has jolted it out of me." "That is a picture of Hawthorne," said Longfellow to a visitor, *Hawthorne.* "as he looked when he was about twenty. He was a shy man, and exceedingly refined. If any one thought he wrote with ease, he should have seen him as I have, seated at a table with pen and paper before him, perfectly still, not writing a word. On one occasion he told me he had been sitting so for hours, waiting for an inspiration to write, meanwhile filled with gloom and an almost apathetic despair." De Tocqueville, at the end of his preface to The Old Régime and the Revolution, says: "I may say, I think, without undue self-laudation, that this book is the fruit of great labor. I could point to more than one short chapter that has cost me more than a year's work." As a commentary on all this, it may be stated that a daughter of Emerson once received a letter from a school-girl, asking for what price her father would write a valedictory address she had to deliver at college! Lamb mentions in one of his Essays having once complained to a schoolmaster that his little sketches were anything but methodical, and that he was unable to make them otherwise, when the wise professor kindly offered to instruct him in the method by which young gentlemen in his seminary were taught to compose English themes! The sister of Hannah More relates that Sterne's daughter — Mrs. Medalle — sent to all the correspondents of her deceased father, begging the letters which he had written to

De Tocqueville.

Sterne's daughter.

them; among other wits, she sent to Wilkes with the same request. He sent for answer, that as there happened to be nothing extraordinary in those he had received, he had burnt or lost them. On which the faithful editor of her father's works sent back to say, that if Mr. Wilkes would be so good as to write a few letters in imitation of her father's style, it would do just as well, and she would insert them! Donald MacLeod, in his Life of Sir Walter Scott, relates that one morning, before breakfast was over (on the occasion of a visit of a distinguished gentleman at Abbotsford), there arrived so mighty a post-bag that the guests in astonishment asked the reason. Scott answered that it was always so, and that although large franking privileges were at his service, his postage bill still amounted to one hundred and fifty pounds annually. He was deluged with all manner of letters. On one occasion, a young lady of New York sent him a manuscript play, called The Cherokee Lovers, requesting him to read and correct it, equip it with prologue and epilogue, bring it out at Drury Lane, and get a handsome price for it from Murray or Constable. Postage, five pounds. In about a fort-

A remarkable request

The Cherokee Lovers.

night, another package arrived, out of which, on being opened, popped another copy of The Cherokees, with another letter, saying that as the winds had been boisterous, she thought that the vessel containing the tragedy might possibly have been foundered, and therefore took the precaution of sending another copy. Postage, five pounds more.

<small>YOUTH AND AGE.</small> Death is as great a wonder to Youth as life is to Age. Youth is ever growing and realizing. His look into the sunless grave is blank and bewildered. His round eyes and radiant face are set upon an upward, sunny path. No blow of disappointment has staggered his expectation, and left an indelible mark upon him. He employs no spies, and advances without scouts. He has not learned the uses of suspicion <small>Effect of easy advancement.</small> and caution. Easy advancement has made him bold and confident. He believes the future is in his fist. He does not know that so far all helps have been supplied him, and will continue to be supplied, till he fails. The fledgeling, left to flutter alone, is hopefully and trustingly observed by those who know forces and currents. Humanity has generously opened a way and

given him a start. His sails belly with all good wishes. The world would not have him fail. It will not give up its faith in its best ideal. Individuals acknowledge they have failed, but they do not quite get their consent to believe that an individual may not exist who cannot fail. If the one well-remembered fatal thing done or omitted had been omitted or done, they might have been such themselves. The possible man who cannot err nor blunder, and who cannot be deceived nor baffled, is the universal Messiah. Wisdom, dumb and grave, and Experience, with doubt and distrust in every wrinkle, forget truth and life, lose themselves in the contemplation of his beautiful vigor and fleetness, and believe him invincible. They look through the past, and see themselves in the fascinating being. Prodigy and miracle. Figure erect, limbs round, veins full and hot, skin glistening, hair shaking out the sunshine. So full of bounding life that his sleep must be disturbed by rapturous dreams of to-morrow. Suggestion of danger in his way would be insufficient to put him on his guard, if time were allowed to hear it. He must learn obstacles by confronting them, and encountering them one at a time, his

The world would not have him fail.

The universal Messiah.

Learns obstacles by confronting them.

strong right arm is strengthened by striking them down. But, one day, Fraud or Conspiracy strikes, and new eyes are suddenly given him. He sees so many doubts and difficulties in his way, that he can hardly determine to move at all. He learns a new language, and applies new names. He discovers motives, and grows dizzy trying to sound them. His anxieties and disappointments are hooks in his side, which turn him over and over in his bed. Abstraction puzzles him. He will be seeing things without their disguises, and the habit affects his character. Dealing so much with shams and devices, he comes to suspect even the genuine and real, and feels daily the gradual decay and death of the ardor, ingenuousness, and confidence which ennobled and inspired the best part of his life. His penetration and sagacious second-sight make him acquainted with the little arts and artifices of his fellows, and he acquires a certain strength and mastery by practicing them. But such a bundle of weaknesses he feels must fall apart. Such an embodiment of frailties, instincts, little qualities, little faculties, and distrust, cannot last. Made up in such great part of what is worn out and worthless, the most natural thing, he thinks, is that it should be transformed into something better, and transported to a condition more favorable to right growth and development.

It is not improbable, if the disposition of a great part of the clergy continues, to give less and less attention to what the world esteems as morals, apart from what they esteem religion, that a system of schools will arise, in which radical morals, as an essential part of religion, will be taught to the people. Attempts to divorce them only tend to weaken and confuse the public conscience, and diminish the influence of spiritual leaders.

SCHOOLS OF MORALS.

The time may come when chairs of common sense will be set up in the universities. The trouble may be to fill them; but suitable men, when wanted, will be found. The distinction between scholarship and usefulness will be better defined. Boys will more and more be educated for the uses of education; and so much that must be unlearned will give place to what may be applied.

CHAIRS OF COMMON SENSE.

SMALL THINGS.

Southey mentions that Dr. Shaw, the naturalist, was one day showing to a friend two volumes written by a Dutchman upon the wings of a butterfly, in the British Museum. "The dissertation is rather voluminous, perhaps you will think," said the enthusiastic naturalist, gravely, "but it is immensely important." "The pursuit of the greatest trifles," said Dr. Cocchi to Spence, "may sometimes have a very good effect: the search after the philosopher's stone has preserved chemistry; and the following astrology so much in former ages, has been the cause of astronomy's being so much advanced in ours. Sir Isaac Newton himself has owned that he began with studying judicial astrology, and that it was his pursuit of that idle and vain study which led him into the beauties of, and love for, astronomy." It has been pronounced a great characteristic of genius to do great things with little means. Paxton could see that so small a matter as a greenhouse could be dilated into a crystal palace, and with two common materials — glass and iron — he raised the palace of the genii; the brightest idea and the noblest ornament added to Europe in this century — the Koh-i-noor of the west.

Newton indebted to astrology.

Livy's definition of Archimedes goes on the same ground. James Watt, when sitting one evening with his aunt, Mrs. Muirhead, at the tea-table, was lectured by her for his idleness. "Take a book," she said, "or do something useful, — you have done nothing for the last hour but to take off the lid of that kettle and put it on again; are you not ashamed of spending your time in this way?" The poor boy had been making experiments on the condensation of steam, now holding a cup, and now a silver spoon over the issuing vapor, and catching and collecting the drops into which it fell. He had at this time obtained the first glimpses of that bright idea which, after making his own fortune, has made the fortunes of thousands — the condensation of steam in a separate vessel. Little creatures, of no real importance but to themselves, get to be sometimes of consideration by what they attach themselves to. "Nature," says Sydney Smith, "descends down to infinite smallness. A great man has his parasites; and if you take a large buzzing blue-bottle fly, and look at it in a microscope, you may see twenty or thirty little ugly insects crawling about it, which, doubtless, think their fly to be the

Watt lectured for his idleness.

Parasites.

bluest, grandest, merriest, most important animal in the universe; and are convinced the world would be at an end if it ceased to buzz." It has been calculated that the insect life upon our globe, if piled in one mass, would exceed in magnitude the heap which would be made by bringing together all the beasts and birds. There is a class of animalcules called Infusoria, because they can be obtained by infusing any vegetable or animal substance in water, which, says Professor Owen, "are the most minute, and apparently the most insignificant of created beings. Many of them are so diminutive that a single drop of water may contain five hundred millions of individuals, a number nearly equaling that of one half of the whole human species now existing upon the surface of the globe." Nevertheless the varieties in size are such that the difference between the smallest and the largest "is greater than that between a mouse and an elephant," though even the elephant of the race is altogether invisible to the naked eye. As to those remarkable sub-soilers, the common earthworms, the ground is almost alive with them. Wherever mould is turned up, it is truly said, there these sappers and miners

Infusoria.

Earthworms.

are turned up with it. They are nature's plowmen. They bore the stubborn soil in every direction, and render it pervious to air, rain, and the fibres of plants. Without these auxiliaries, "the farmer," says Gilbert White, "would find that his land would become cold, hard-bound, and sterile." The green mantle of vegetation which covers the earth is dependent upon the worms which burrow in the bowels of it. What conveys a more definite idea of the magnitude of their operations, they are perpetually replenishing the upper soil, and covering with soft and fine material a crust which before was close and ungenial. They swallow a quantity of earth with their food, and having extracted the nutriment they eject the remainder at the outlet of their holes. This refuse forms the worm-casts which are the annoyance of the gardener, who might be reconciled to them if he were aware that the depositors save him a hundred times more labor than they cause. Mr. Charles Darwin has shown that in thirteen years a field of pasture was covered to a depth of three inches and a half with the mould discharged from their intestines, and in another case the layer they had accumulated in eighty years

Nature's plowmen.

Replenishing the upper soil.

Statement of Darwin's.

was from twelve to fourteen inches thick. They therefore play a most important part in the economy of vegetation, and we see why they teem throughout the surface of the globe. "I was told," says Lady Mary Wortley Montagu, "by a very good author, who is deep in the secret, that at this very minute there is a bill cooking up at a hunting-seat in Norfolk, to have 'not' taken out of the Commandments, and clapped into the Creed, the ensuing season of Parliament. This bold attempt for the liberty of the subject is wholly projected by Mr. Walpole, who proposed it to the secret committee in his parlor. William Young seconded it, and answered for all his acquaintances voting right to a man. Doddington very gravely objected that the obstinacy of human nature was such that he feared when they had positive commands to do so perhaps people would not commit adultery and bear false witness against their neighbors with the readiness and cheerfulness they do at present. This objection seemed to sink deep into the minds of the great politicians at the boards, and I don't know whether the bill won't be dropped." Goethe's connection with the Weimar theatre, it is said, was finally and

The little word "not."

Doddington's objection.

wholly broken off by means of a dog and a mistress. One Karsten possessed a performing poodle, and traveled about with this intelligent animal, representing a certain melodrama. The pampered and petted Von Heygendorff bore a spite against the inflexible director, and, with feminine malice, she, in order to annoy Goethe, induced her lover, the duke, to consent to an engagement of Karsten and his dog. Goethe at once resigned, and the duke accepted the resignation. He afterwards withdrew his acceptance, but Goethe remained proudly inflexible; and the classic epoch of the Weimar theatre was terminated by a clever and unconscious poodle, who emulated the mischief produced by Newton's dog Diamond. It is related that when Layard, the discoverer of Nineveh, was twenty years old and lounging through Mesopotamia he was captured by an Arab tribe and made the chief's cook, in which position he was greatly admired, and called by the women of the tribe "the blue-eyed." He did not enjoy his slavery, and after a while managed to communicate with his friends, and at the end of a good deal of talk the Arab chief consented to exchange his prisoner for a greyhound, celebrated in

A dog and a mistress.

Goethe inflexible.

Layard.

the country for hunting gazelles. His first halt on his return to civilization was at the encampment of Botta, who had been making longitudinal excavations, and to his despair without result. Layard was struck by a clever idea — to cut transversely. This was done, and Nineveh was discovered. That happy thought decided his vocation — he became an archæologist. "The only memory I don't like," said Layard, gayly, "is that I was exchanged for a dog. My only consolation is in the fact that a Selongui greyhound is considered by Mussulmans as an especially noble animal." The foolish ballad of Lilli Burlero, treating the Papists, and chiefly the Irish, in a very ridiculous manner, slight and insignificant as it now seems, had once a more powerful effect than the Philippics of either Demosthenes or Cicero; it contributed not a little toward the great revolution in 1688; the whole army and the people in country and city caught it up, and "sang a deluded prince out of three kingdoms." The air is gay and beautiful; it is one of the masterpieces of Purcell, and lingers in the ear of every person who has once heard it. No wonder My Uncle Toby adopted it as a favorite and resource. Strahan, the

Nineveh discovered.

Effect of a ballad.

printer, and friend of Johnson, once observed that many men were kept back from trying their fortunes in London because they were born to a competency, and said, "Small certainties are the bane of men of talents." "Small debts," said Johnson, "are like small shot; they are rattling on every side, and can scarcely be escaped without a wound: great debts are like cannon; of loud noise, but little danger. You must, therefore, be enabled to discharge petty debts, that you may have leisure, with security, to struggle with the rest." A gentleman visited Gibson, the sculptor, not long before his death, when he found him busy with his beautiful Pandora — finished, as it seemed, but still "in the clay." There she stood — a model of refined grace — her box in her hand. The old man sat before it, talking and philosophizing. As he talked, he would gaze at his figure and, wetting his finger, would now and again pass it down the surface of a limb, giving a faint depression, or scraping off a film as faint. "Bless you," he said, "there's a month's work on it yet!" Reminding one of the saying of the old Greek sculptor, answering his objector that these were trifles. "Trifles make per-

Small certainties.

Figure of Pandora.

fection, and perfection is no trifle." Ah! trifles! "How much wiser," exclaimed Lady Mary Montagu, "are all those women I have despised than myself! In placing their happiness in trifles, they have placed it in what is attainable."

<small>SECTS AND CREEDS.</small> Bayle in his Dictionary tells us that the sect which pleased Milton most in his youth was that of the Puritans; but in his middle age he was best pleased with the Independents and Anabaptists, because they allowed more liberty to every private person, and in his opinion seemed to come nearest to the primitive Christians: but in the latter part of his life he separated himself from all communions, and did not frequent any Christian assembly, nor made use of their peculiar rites in his family. As for the rest, he expressed the profoundest reverence to God as well in deeds as words. It has been very justly said that the whole tangle of authoritative creeds <small>*The tangle embarrassing.*</small> is, at the best, embarrassing. They lead a man, from their nature, to try to continue in a belief which he once thought he had. They give a fossil form to what should be pliant, elastic, and alive. I believe, said Dean Swift, that thousands of men would

be orthodox enough in certain points, if divines had not been too curious, or too narrow, in reducing orthodoxy within the compass of subtleties, niceties, and distinctions, with little warrant from Scripture, and less from reason or good policy. When Theodore Hook, in the old days of the English test oath, was asked if he could swear to the XXXIX articles, he replied, "Certainly, with all my heart; I am only sorry there are not more of them." Love, in the judgment of Hunt, is the only creed destined to survive all others. "They who think that no church can exist without a strong spice of terror, should watch the growth of education, and see which system of it is most beloved. They should see, also, which system in the very nursery is growing the most ridiculous."

Divines too curious, or too narrow.

The creed destined to survive.

A late commentator upon Goethe's Faust is free to express the opinion that "evil, as a stimulant to deed, to creative activity, is an element of progress; as selfish indulgence, producing indolence and intellectual inactivity, tends downward, and causes cessation of spiritual life. It is in this respect comparable to poisons which in certain solutions stimulate the

Good out of Evil.

vital forces of the human system and are useful as medicines, while in their undiluted state they have the directly opposite effect, causing instant cessation of the animal life. If there are material things which have this double action upon the physical system, may there not be moral agencies, too, that have analogous effects upon the moral system?" Southey, in one of his attractive biographies, tells us how Louis XIV. "by one wicked edict revoked the privileges of the French Protestants, and by another of the same day prohibited their public worship, banished their ministers, and decreed that their children should be educated by Roman Catholic priests in the Roman Catholic faith; the better to insure obedience he quartered dragoons upon them, and left them to the mercy of his military missionaries. The Dragonnades, as they were called, were a fit afterpiece to the tragedy of St. Bartholomew's day. The number of persons who emigrated in consequence of this execrable persecution has been variously computed from fifty to five hundred thousand; more meritorious men were never driven from their native country, and every country which afforded them refuge was amply re-

Material things and moral agencies

The Dragonnades.

warded by their talents, their arts, and their industry. Prussia received a large and most beneficial increase of useful subjects; they multiplied the looms of England, and gave new activity to the trade of Holland. Some of these refugees converted rocks into vineyards on the shores of the Leman Lake; and British Africa is indebted to others for wines which will one day rival those of the Rhine and the Garonne." Few men were more bigoted or cruel than Archbishop Laud. He sharpened the spiritual sword, and drew it against all sorts of offenders, intending that the discipline of the church should be felt as well as spoken of. There had not been such a crowd of business in the High Commission Court since the Reformation, nor so many large fines imposed, as under the prelate's administration. The fines, we are told, were assigned to the repairs of St. Paul's, which gave rise to the proverb, that "the church was repaired with the sins of the people." *[Effect of emigration. Cruelty and bigotry of Laud.]*

John Wesley, according to his best biographer, related remarkable cures wrought by his faith and his prayers, which he considered, and represented, as positively *[THE FAITH CURE.]*

miraculous. By thinking strongly on a text of Scripture which promised that these signs should follow those that believe, and by calling on Christ to increase his faith and confirm the word of his grace, he shook off instantaneously, he says, a fever which had hung upon him for some days, and was in a moment freed from all pain, and restored to his former strength. He visited a believer at night who was not expected to live till the morning: the man was speechless and senseless, and his pulse gone. "A few of us," says Wesley, "immediately joined in prayers. I relate the naked fact. Before we had done, his senses and his speech returned. Now, he that will account for this by natural causes has my free leave. But I choose to say this is the power of God." So, too, when his own teeth ached, he prayed, and the pain left him. And this faith was so strong, that it sufficed to cure, not only himself, but his horse also. "My horse," he says, "was so exceedingly lame, that I was afraid I must have lain by. We could not discern what it was that was amiss, and yet he could scarce set his foot to the ground. By riding thus seven miles I was thoroughly tired, and my head ached more than it had done

In a moment freed from all pain.

Cured his horse also.

for some months. What I here aver is the naked fact: let every man account for it as he sees good. I then thought, 'Cannot God heal either man or beast, by any means, or without any?' Immediately my weariness and headache ceased, and my horse's lameness in the same instant. Nor did he halt any more either that day or the next."

It is related that Scott, while attending Dugald Stewart's lectures on moral philosophy, sat often beside a person considerably older than himself — of a very humble rank, apparently, but of great diligence in his studies. Scott paid him some attention, and they contracted quite an intimacy, and used to take walks together; but the young man never spoke of his parentage or residence. One day Scott stopped to relieve a bluegown, or licensed beggar, who stood hat in hand, silently leaning on his staff. This happened three or four times, and Scott was beginning to get acquainted with the old man, when, one day, he met him in company with his fellow-student, who showed some confusion. "Do you know anything to the old man's discredit?" asked Walter. "Oh, no, sir;

POVERTY.

A bluegown.

God forbid!" cried the poor fellow, bursting into tears; "but I am a poor wretch to be ashamed to speak to him. He is my own father! He has enough laid by to serve him in his old age; but he stands there, bleaching his head in the wind, that he may get the means of paying for my education!" True enough is the exclamation of Dickens, in Bleak House, "What the poor are to the poor, is little known, excepting to themselves and God." "Poverty," says Plutarch, "is not dishonorable in itself, but only when it arises from idleness, intemperance, extravagance, and folly." "An avowal of poverty is a disgrace to no man; to make no effort to escape from it is indeed disgraceful," is a saying of Thucydides. When Faustine, in Hugo's masterpiece, saw that she could live by her small wages, she had a moment of joy. To live honestly by her own toil, what a favor of Heaven! There is a passage of vivid description in one of Dickens' stories — who could forget it? "In a small English country town, the inhabitants of which supported themselves by the labor of their hands in plaiting and preparing straw for those who made bonnets and other articles of dress and ornament

An exclamation of Dickens'.

Faustine's moment of joy.

from that material — concealed under an assumed name, and living in a quiet poverty which knew no change, no pleasures, and few cares but that of struggling on from day to day in the one great toil for bread — dwelt Barnaby and his mother." *Barnaby and his mother.* Johnson, giving expression to his own wretched experience, wrote from time to time to Boswell, "Poverty, my dear friend, is so great an evil, and pregnant with so much temptation, and so much misery, that I cannot but earnestly enjoin you to avoid it. Live on what you have; live if you can on less; do not borrow either for vanity or pleasure; the vanity will end in shame, and the pleasure in regret; stay therefore at home, till you have saved money for your journey hither. Do not accustom yourself to consider debt only as an inconvenience; you will find it a calamity. Poverty takes away so many means of doing good, and produces so much inability to resist evil, both natural and moral, that it is by all virtuous means to be *By all virtuous means to be avoided.* avoided. Consider a man whose fortune is very narrow; whatever his rank by birth, or whatever his reputation by intellectual excellence, what can he do? or what evil can he prevent? That he cannot help the needy, is evident; he has nothing to spare. But, perhaps, his advice or admonition may be useful. His poverty will destroy his influence; many more can find that he is poor, than that he is wise; and few will reverence the understanding that is of so little advantage to its owner. Resolve not to be poor; whatever you have, spend less. Poverty is a great enemy to human happiness; it certainly destroys liberty, and it makes some virtues impracticable, and others extremely difficult. No man can help others that wants help himself; we must have enough before we have to spare. I remember, and entreat you to remember, that the first approach to riches is security from poverty." The saying of Socrates, that "he who wants least is most like the gods, who want nothing," was a favorite sentence with Johnson. Fortunately, the necessaries of life do not cost much, or the poor could not live.

Whatever you have, spend less.

"The laws of nature teach us exactly what we need," says Montaigne. "After the sages have told us that according to nature no one is indigent, and that every one is so according to opinion, they very subtly distinguish between the desires that proceed from her and those that proceed from

Nature teaches what we need.

the disorder of our own fancy; those of which we can see the end are hers; those that fly from us, and of which we can see no end, are our own. Want of goods is easily repaired; poverty of soul is irreparable." Adversity has been called the trial of principle. Without it a man hardly knows whether he is an honest man. "However mean your life is, meet it and live it," says Thoreau; "do not shun it and call it hard names. It is not as bad as you are. It looks poorest when you are richest. The fault-finder will find faults even in paradise. Love your life, poor as it is. You may perhaps have some pleasant, thrilling, glorious hours, even in a poor-house. The setting sun is reflected from the windows of the almshouse as brightly as from the rich man's abode; the snow melts before its door as early in the spring. I do not see but a quiet mind may live as contentedly there, and have as cheering thoughts, as in a palace. The town's poor seem to me often to live the most independent lives of any. May be they are simply great enough to receive without misgiving. Most think that they are above being supported by the town; but it often happens that they are not

Adversity the trial of principle.

The town's poor.

above supporting themselves by dishonest means, which should be more disreputable. Cultivate poverty like a garden herb, like sage. Do not trouble yourselves much to get new things, whether clothes or friends. Turn the old; return to them. Things do not change; we change. Sell your clothes and keep your thoughts. God will see that you do not want society." "O, beloved and gentle Poverty!" exclaims Souvestre's philosopher in his attic; "pardon me for having for a moment wished to fly from thee, as I would from Want; stay here forever with thy charming sisters, Pity, Patience, Sobriety, and Solitude; be ye my queens and my instructors; teach me the stern duties of life; remove far from my abode the weakness of heart, and giddiness of head which follow prosperity. Holy Poverty! teach me to endure without complaining, to impart without grudging, to seek the end of life higher than in pleasure, farther off than in power. Thou givest the body strength, thou makest the mind more firm; and, thanks to thee, this life, to which the rich attach themselves as to a rock, becomes a bark of which death may cut the cable without awakening all our fears. Continue to sustain me, O thou whom Christ hath called Blessed." "O hunger, hunger, immortal hunger!" apostrophizes John Buncle. "Thou art the blessing of the poor, the regale of the temperate rich, and the delicious gust of the plainest morsel. Cursed is the man that has turned thee out-of-doors, and at whose table thou art a stranger! Yea, thrice cursed is he, who always thirsts, and hungers no more!" Poverty, or rather indifference to worldly wealth, is that which Renan claims to have most faithfully practiced. "My dream," he says, "would be to be lodged, fed, clothed, and warmed, without having to bestow a thought about it, by somebody who would take me by contract and leave me to do what I pleased." Phædrus relates, in one of his fables, that when Hercules was received into heaven, and was saluting the gods who thronged around with their congratulations, he turned away his look when Plutus drew near, assigning as a reason for this to Jupiter, who inquired the cause of his strange conduct, that he hated Plutus because he was a friend to the bad; and, besides, corrupted both good and bad with his gifts. As to low living and high thinking, so often extolled by the philosophers

Hunger apostrophized.

Renan's dream.

Hercules and Plutus

—a careless concern for the things of this world and a pitch of excellence sublimely superhuman — they are not without their provoking inconveniences and melancholy effects, as examples prove. Cardell Goodman and Benjamin Griffin, both good actors long after Shakespeare, shared, we are told, the same bed in their modest lodging, and having but one shirt between them, wore it each in his turn. The only dissension which ever occurred between them was caused by Goodman, who, having to pay a visit to a lady, clapped on the shirt when it was clean, and Griffin's day for wearing it! "Edgar A. Poe I remember seeing on a single occasion," writes the author of Memories of Many Men and Some Women. "He announced a lecture to be delivered at the Society Library building on Broadway, under the title of The Universe. It was a stormy night, and there were not more than sixty persons present in the lecture-room. I have seen no portrait of Poe that does justice to his pale, delicate, intellectual face and magnificent eyes. His lecture was a rhapsody of the most intense brilliancy. He appeared inspired, and his inspiration affected the scant audience almost painfully. He wore

Two good actors.

Poe's lecture on The Universe.

his coat tightly buttoned across his slender chest; his eyes seemed to glow like those of his own raven, and he kept us entranced for two hours and a half. The late Mr. Putnam, the publisher, told me that the next day the wayward, luckless poet presented himself to him with the manuscript of The Universe. He told Putnam that in it he solved the whole problem of life; that it would immortalize its publisher as well as its author; and, what was of less consequence, that it would bring to him the fortune which he had so long and so vainly been seeking. Mr. Putnam, while an admirer of genius, was also a cool, calculating man of business. As such, he could not see the matter in exactly the same light as the poet did, and the only result of the interview was that he lent Poe a shilling to take him home to Fordham, where he then resided."

His eyes glowed like his own raven's.

Readers of Dickens will remember Georgiana Pocket — a cousin of Miss Havisham's — an indigestive single woman, who called her rigidity religion, and her liver love. It is Emerson, I believe, who speaks of brains paralyzed by stomach. He says also that he knew a witty phy-

DIGESTION.

sician who found the creed in the biliary duct, and used to affirm that if there was disease in the liver, the man became a Calvinist, and if that organ was sound, he became a Unitarian. "Much wisdom in olives," said Sancho Panza. "Soup and fish," in the judgment of Sydney Smith, "explain half of the emotions of life." You remember the account Swedenborg has left us of his first vision: "I had eaten a hearty supper, perhaps too hearty: and I was sitting alone in my chair, when a bright being suddenly appeared to me, and said, 'Swedenborg, why hast thou eaten too much?'" Voltaire was ashamed of his indigestion. He wrote to Madame de Bernières, "I am ashamed to present myself to my friends with a weak digestion and a downcast mind. I wish to give you only my beautiful days, and to suffer incognito." Rumford, it is said, proposed to the elector of Bavaria a scheme for feeding his soldiers at a much cheaper rate than formerly. His plan was simply to compel them to masticate their food thoroughly. A small quantity, thus eaten, would, according to that famous projector, afford more sustenance than a large meal hastily devoured. "I do not know," remarks Ma-

The liver.

A bright being appeared to Swedenborg.

Rumford's scheme.

caulay, "how Rumford's proposition was received; but to the mind, I believe, it will be found more nutritious to digest a page than to devour a volume."

Montenegro has hardly any plains. The limestone ridges of the Dinaric Alps which traverse it, occasionally diversified by lofty peaks, are so rugged and rocky that the people have the common saying: "When God was in the act of distributing stones over the earth, the bag that held them burst, and let them all fall upon Montenegro." Death in battle is regarded by them as natural death, but death in bed as something apart from nature. The women, we are told, have the same passionate attachment with the men to family and country, and display much of the same valor. Gladstone has given two most remarkable examples, supplied by Goptchevitch. A sister and four brothers, the four of course all armed, are making a pilgrimage or excursion to a church. The state of war with the Turk being normal, we need not wonder when we learn that they are attacked unawares on their way, in a pass where they proceed in single file, by seven armed Turks; who announce themselves

Heroism

Example of valor.

by shooting dead the first of the brothers, and dangerously wounding the second. *Odds fearful, but the fight proceeds.* The odds are fearful, but the fight proceeds. The wounded man leans against the rock, and though he receives another and fatal shot, kills two of the Turks before he dies. The sister presses forward, and grasps his rifle and his dagger. At last all are killed on both sides, excepting herself and a single Turk. She asks for mercy; and he promises it, but names her maidenly honor as the price. Indignant, and perceiving that now he is off his guard, she stabs him with the dagger. He tears it from her hand, they close, and she dashes the wretch over the precipice into the yawning depth below. *Another remarkable example.* The second instance is quite as remarkable. Tidings reach a Montenegrin wife that her husband has just been slain by a party under the command of a certain Turkish officer. Knowing the road by which they are traveling, she seizes a rifle, chooses her position, and shoots the officer dead. The rest of the party take to flight. *The widow's challenge.* The wife of the dead Turk sends the Montenegrin widow an epistle. "Thou hast robbed me of both my eyes. Thou art a genuine daughter of Tscernagora. Come to-morrow alone to the border-line, and we will prove by trial which was the better wife." The Tscernagorine appeared, equipped with the arms of the dead Turkish officer, and alone, as she was invited. But the Turkish woman had thought prudence the better part of valor, and brought an armed champion with her, who charged her on horseback. She shot him dead as he advanced, and seizing her faithless antagonist, bound her and took her home, kept her as a nurse-maid for fourteen years, and then let her go back to her place and people.

It is a maxim, that character and destiny are the same thing. "Be what you were meant to be," said one of the Concord philosophers. "You may go through the world an oddity, to your own merriment at least, if not that of your contemporaries. Character is a fact, and that is much in a world of pretense and concession. Character, not accomplishments, but character personally controlling these, does the work. Manners carry the world for the moment, character for all times. Your real influence is measured by your treatment of yourself. First find the man in yourself if you will inspire manliness in others. Like begets

CHARACTER.

Manners for the moment, character for all times.

like the world over." "Take the place and attitude," says Emerson, "which belong to you, and all men acquiesce. The world must be just. It leaves every man with profound unconcern, to set his own rate." Schiller, in Wallenstein, affirms that "Every man stamps his value on himself. The price we challenge for ourselves is given us. There does not live on earth the man, be his station what it may, that I despise myself compared with him. Man is made great or little by his own will." Thoreau insists, in his vigorous way, that "Every man should stand for a force which is perfectly irresistible. How can any man be weak who dares to be at all? Even the tenderest plants force their way up through the hardest earth, and the crevices of rocks; but a man no material power can resist. What a wedge, what a beetle, what a catapult, is an earnest man! What can resist him?" Yet, says Mill, "It is individuality that we war against: we should think we had done wonders if we had made ourselves all alike; forgetting that the unlikeness of one person to another is generally the first thing which draws the attention of either to the imperfection of his own type, and the superiority of another, or the possi-

The world must be just.

Yet we war against individuality.

bility, by combining the advantages of both, of producing something better than either." "Common natures," said Lamb, "do not suffice me. Good people, as they are called, won't serve me. I want individuals. I am made up of queer points, and I want so many answering needles." Of self-development, Maudsley says, there is hardly any one who sets it before himself as an aim in life. "The question to be entertained and decided at the outset will be, whether this aim shall be internal or external — whether the individual shall seek first the completest development of which his nature is capable, other gains, such as riches, reputation, power, being allowed to fall to him by the way; or whether he shall seek worldly success, the formation of character being allowed to be a secondary and incidental matter? The formation of character in which the thoughts, feelings, and actions are under the habitual guidance of a well fashioned will, is perhaps the hardest task in the world, being, when accomplished, the highest effort of self-development. It represents the attainment by conscious method of a harmony of the individual nature in itself, and of the completest harmony between man and nature; a condition in which the individual has succceded in making the best of himself, of the human nature with which he has to do, and of the world in which he moves and has his being." Froude says, writing of Cicero, *Manner and character.* "A man's own manner and character is what best becomes him." "In Carlyle as in Byron," said Emerson, "one is more struck with the rhetoric than with the matter. He has manly superiority rather than intellectuality, and so makes good hits all the time. There is more character than intellect in every sentence, herein strongly resembling Samuel Johnson." George Eliot wrote in her Diary, "I have seen Emerson — I have seen a man." When Jenny Lind was in Boston, Mr. Webster called upon her. When he was gone, she jumped up, walked the floor excitedly, clasped her hands, and with indescribable earnestness exclaimed, "Oh, that is a man! that is a man! I never saw a man before! I never saw a man before!" *Tranquillity.* Madame de Maintenon pronounced tranquillity the supreme power. When Nelson had finished his famous dispatch to the Crown Prince of Denmark, at the battle of Copenhagen, a wafer was given him to seal it with; but he ordered a candle to be brought from the cock-pit, and sealed the letter with wax, affixing a larger seal than he ordinarily used. "This," remarked he, "is no time to appear hurried or informal."

"I remember a small Mussulman boy," says an officer, in his published Recollections of Military Service in India, "one of our servants, lying on the veranda, apparently asleep, when, to our horror, we saw a cobra creep out of a lot of boots, lying near, which the boy had been cleaning. The cobra passed over his face, and actually darted his tongue in and out of his open mouth. The boy never stirred, and we remarked how providential it was that he was fast asleep. The snake after a time glided off, when the boy jumped up, and seized a stick, and killed it. He had been awake all the time." Thoreau asks, "Which would have advanced the most at the end of a month, — the boy who had made his own jackknife from the ore which he had dug and smelted, reading as much as would be necessary for this, — or the boy who had attended the lectures on metallurgy at the Institute in the mean while, and had received a Rogers penknife from his father? Which would be most

The Mussulman boy and the cobra.

Had been awake all the time.

likely to cut his fingers?" Character and powers, early and late, do not much vary. The inspiration of purpose, and work, very

Personality. soon establish personality. Can any man remember when the radically distinguishing things he stands for first took root within him? Nathaniel Hawthorne, when he was sixteen years old, sent forth, we are told, the first number of The Spectator, a small but neatly printed and well edited paper. A prospectus had been issued only the week before, setting forth that The Spectator would be issued on Wednesdays, "price twelve cents per annum, payment to be made at the end of the year." Among the advertisements on the last page was this: "Nathaniel Hawthorne proposes to publish, by subscription, a neat edition of The Miseries of Authors, to which will be added a sequel containing facts and remarks drawn from his own experience." The Hawthorne of The Scarlet

An oration by Daniel Webster. Letter already existed. An oration delivered by Daniel Webster July 4, 1802, — then twenty years old, and principal of Fryeburg Academy, — was recently discovered in a mass of the author's private papers which had found their way into a junk shop. The last speech made by Mr.

Webster in the Senate of the United States, July 17, 1850, concluded with the same peroration with which he closed the Fryeburg oration, forty-eight years before! I like to repeat the words that young Thomas Carlyle wrote to his brother, nine years after he had left the University of Edinburgh as a student, forty-three years before he returned as its rector. "I say, Jack, thou and I must never falter. Work, my boy, work unweariedly. I swear that all the thousand miseries of this hard fight, and ill-health, the most terrific of them all, shall never chain us down. By the river Styx it shall not. Two fellows from a nameless spot in Annandale shall yet show the world the pluck that is in the Carlyles." That mighty hater and smiter of cant and shams was of good Scotch stock, and had been generously brought up on good air, simple food, and sound instruction. The qualities that he had inherited and scrupulously cultivated were genuine, and of the highest manhood. The "pith o' sense," and "pride o' worth," and books, made him so much a man, and so different from other men, that independence was necessary to him. If he was to be a man, and fight the battle of life on his own ground, it must

Carlyle.

Independence necessary to him.

be his, without any question of title. Believing that in the hour in which a man "mortgages himself to two, or ten, or twenty, he dwarfs himself below the stature of one;" and being determined that he would not be "cramped and diminished of his proportions," the desire, not for riches, but for independence, took deep root within him. He felt that he had much to say in this world, and would say it, without favor or fear. It is true, as a quaint old writer puts it, that the greatest part of our felicity is to be well-born — of parents, in other words, of sound bodies, sound minds, and correct principles, and to inherit the same. Especially, if it be true, as Hazlitt asserts, that "no one ever changes his character from the time he is two years old; nay, from the time he is two hours old. We may, with instruction and opportunity, mend our manners, or else alter them for the worse, 'as the flesh or fortune shall serve;' but the character, the internal original bias remains always the same, true to itself to the very last — 'and feels the ruling passion strong in death.' The color of our lives is woven into the fatal thread at our births; our original sins and our redeeming graces

The desire took deep root within him.

The internal original bias.

are infused into us; nor is the bond, that confirms our destiny, ever canceled." Inheritance is fate. The stuff of manhood in Daniel Webster, when he was briefless and penniless, led him to decline a clerkship of two thousand a year — feeling it to be his mission "to make opinions for other men to record, and not to be the clerk to record the opinions of courts." It is related that when he, in attacking a legal proposition of an opponent at the bar, was reminded that he was assailing a dictum of Lord Camden, he turned to the court, and after paying a tribute to Camden's greatness, as a jurist, simply added, "But, may it please your Honor, I differ from Lord Camden." It is evident that such self-assertion would have been ridiculous had not the character of the man relieved it from all essential pretension. Judge Story, on the evening previous to the delivery of the great speech in reply to Hayne, called on Mr. Webster, and, after expressing some anxiety as to the result of the debate, offered to aid him in looking up materials. Mr. Webster thanked him, and said, "Give yourself no uneasiness, Judge Story; I will grind him as fine as a pinch of snuff." It is said that when Thorwaldsen, the Danish

Inheritance is fate.

Reply to Hayne.

sculptor, saw Webster's head in Powers' studio in Rome, he exclaimed, "Ah! a design for Jupiter, I see!" He would not believe that it was a living American. Theodore Parker describes him as "a man of large mould, a great body and a great brain. Since Socrates there has seldom been a head so massive, so huge. Its cubic capacity surpassed all former measurements of mind. A large man, decorous in dress, dignified in deportment, he walked as if he felt himself a king. Men from the country, who knew him not, stared at him as he passed through Boston streets. The coal-heavers and porters of London looked on him as one of the great forces of the globe. They recognized in him a native king." Carlyle, in a letter to Emerson, called him a magnificent specimen; "as a logic-fencer, advocate, or parliamentary Hercules, one would incline to back him at first sight against all the extant world." Sydney Smith pronounced him "a living lie; because no man on earth could be as great as he looked." An eminent contemporary has written: "There was a certain grandeur in Webster's look which was incomparable. His Olympian presence gave an air of significance and dignity to whatever he said. I have heard him deliver the most astonishing commonplaces in such a way that the audience seemed to be listening to a new revelation of great truths." Hawthorne, after viewing Powers' colossal statue of Webster, wrote in his Note-Book: "There is an expression of quiet, solid, massive strength in the whole figure; a deep pervading energy, in which any exaggeration of gesture would lessen and lower the effect. He looks really like a pillar of the state. The face is very grand, very Webster; stern and awful, because he is in the act of meeting a great crisis, and yet with the warmth of a great heart glowing through it. Happy is Webster to have been so truly and adequately sculptured; happy the sculptor in such a subject, which no idealization of a demigod could have supplied him with. Perhaps the statue at the bottom of the sea will be cast up in some future age, when the present race of man is forgotten, and if so, that far posterity will look up to us as a grander race than we find ourselves to be." What a thing to be a man! Who, worth his bread, has not aspired to recognized manhood and absolute personal freedom? "I would not," said Othello, "my unhoused,

Effect of Webster's Olympian presence.

What a thing to be a man!

free condition put into circumspection and confine for the sea's worth." He has been decided a lucky fox that left his tail in the trap. The muskrat, observed Thoreau, would gnaw his third leg off to be free. The human race, its whole history proves, prefers struggle to dependence, as horses prefer the wild plain to the stall. There is a remarkable bird called the Quetzal — a native of Guatemala — a curious creature — resembling a parrot, and is so constituted that if but one of its feathers is plucked it instantly dies. If an attempt is made to cage this strange feathered visitant, it deliberately attempts suicide by pulling out its own feathers, preferring death to captivity. One of these birds was shown at the New Orleans Exhibition in the winter of 1884-5. Fénelon wrote, in a letter to one of his friends, "It is only upon a very small number of true friends that I count, and I do it not from motives of interest, but from pure esteem ; not from a desire to derive any advantage from them, but to do them justice in not distrusting their affection. I would like to oblige the whole human race, especially virtuous people ; but there is scarcely anybody to whom I would like to be under obligation. Is it through

Struggle preferable to dependence.

Fénelon to one of his friends.

haughtiness and pride that I think thus? Nothing could be more foolish and more unbecoming; but I have learned to know men as I have grown old, and believe that it is the best way to do without them, without pretending to superior wisdom." Pope Clement the Sixth offered to Petrarch not only the office of Apostolic Secretary, but many considerable bishoprics. Petrarch constantly refused them. "You will not accept of anything I offer you!" said the Holy Father: "Ask of me what you please." Two months afterwards Petrarch *Petrarch.* wrote to one of his friends: "Every degree of elevation creates new suspicions in my mind, because I perceive the misfortunes that attend them. Would they but grant me that happy mediocrity so preferable to *Preferred mediocrity* gold, and which they have promised me, I *to gold.* should accept the gift with gratitude and cordiality; but if they only intend to invest me with some important employment, I should refuse it. I will shake off the yoke; for I had much rather live poor than become a slave."

"Uncle," said Walter Gay to Captain The Hope Cuttle, gayly, laying his hand upon the old man's shoulder, "what shall I send you home from Barbados?" "Hope, my dear Wally. Hope ... Send me as much of that as you can." How short would life be if hope did not prolong it, is an Arabic maxim. Alas, in the Tamil language (it is said) there is no word for it. "Hast thou hope?" they asked of John Knox when dying. He said nothing, but raised his finger and pointed upwards. Lamartine, in Raphael, says of one of his characters: "There was but one thing grieved me as I looked at him — it was, to see him advancing towards death without believing in immortality. The natural sciences that he had so deeply studied had accustomed his mind to trust exclusively to the evidence of his senses. Nothing existed for him that was not palpable; what could not be calculated contained no element of certitude in his eyes; matter and figures composed his universe; numbers were his god; the phenomena of nature were his revelations; nature being his Bible and his gospel; his virtue was instinct — not seeing that numbers, phenomena, nature, and virtue are but hieroglyphs inscribed on the veil of the temple, whose unanimous meaning is — Deity. Sublime but stubborn minds, who wonderfully ascend the steps of science, one by one, — but will never pass the last, which leads to God." It is now a good many years since I found myself walking on a solitary country road with a scientist of considerable distinction. It was, I think, late in December. The mercury was many degrees below freezing. It was with the utmost difficulty that we escaped suffering by rapid walking. A deep snow covered everything. The road, even, was white like the fields, and the crushed crystals under our feet gave the accustomed resentful complaint. The cloudless expanse of heaven seemed colder than the earth beneath — a very firmament of pellucid ice. Some winter birds, we observed, had bunched themselves on twigs, and were as motionless and still as if they had grown there. The only creature on the wing was a lustrous great crow, which flew uncertainly, as if lost or bewildered. Its plumage had a supernatural icy glitter. No sound was distinctly audible but of our own voices, and of the snow under our feet, except the pitiful wail of an infant, as it came to us appealingly over the frozen fields. Arctic as could be was everything — above, below, on every side — and the scene infixed itself ineffaceably in my mem-

On a solitary country road.

Arctic was everything.

ory. The conversation had become grave, and the tendency to despairing views was momentarily increasing. The dead season was in its shroud. The bitter experiences and pitiful limitations of life were remarked upon, and the infinite discouragements to effort. The little that we achieved seemed the least that was possible. The inevitable difficulties of the human lot were so discouraging and obstructive, if not overwhelming. So much of the little that we know is acquired only by suffering and blundering. Our passions so often commit us to a blind undertaking of the impossible. In certain moods, it seemed the most natural thing in the world that we should view it all as an inexplicable enigma, and ourselves as an insignificant part of it. The hope of a better condition seemed to me the only inspiration to carry us through this. In the logic of things, to say nothing of Scripture, there must be something better. It is not natural to die in infancy; and what could be much more immature than the wisest human being? This must be but a beginning. It must be that here we only begin to be what we are to be. Would a wise man, as we understand wisdom, arrange a vast scheme of difficulty

The dead season in its shroud.

This but a beginning.

and suffering, with nothing worthily compensating to come of it? A brighter day will succeed the darkness, and a better and perpetual growth have a beginning, as the bursting and rejoicing spring with its revivifying sunshine, its green mantle, its roses, its song, will follow the disheartening winter, — to bloom in the never-ending procession — the everlasting progress of nature. Simonides was right, I think, in calling the human skull the shell of the flown bird. "Infatuation! credulity! Pardon me!" exclaimed the scientist, as we turned about, stopped, and faced each other on the bleak road. "Your view is the popular one, I admit, and I do not antagonize it; but mine is the opposite — a conclusion founded in reason, and I can see no other which is scientific, logical, or tenable." "What!" said I, in astonishment. "You do not believe in a perpetuity of existence?" "I do not, most assuredly." "That death ends all?" — repeating the phrase interrogatively, and looking him doubtingly in the face. "Not the shadow of a doubt of it." "Nothing to survive this poor human body?" "Nothing!" was the deliberate reply, — with a coldness and hopelessness more chilling than the

A brighter day to succeed the darkness.

The scientist's conclusion.

frigid atmosphere about us, and my inmost soul — the immortal thinking and hoping part of me — in every faculty and quality of it — shivered at the bold scientist's conclusion. The little unmistakable, almost inaudible cough that the doomed man had been fighting on the way, with drops and lozenges, seemed feebly to echo or mock the irreversible dictum, and kept me lamenting the inconceivable desolation of a human heart without a hope of a future existence. "Everything is prospective," wrote Emerson, "and man is to live hereafter. That the world is for his education is the only sane solution of the enigma. We must infer our destiny from the preparation. We are driven by instinct to hive innumerable experiences which are of no visible value, and we may revolve through many lives before we shall assimilate or exhaust them. Shall I hold on with both hands to every paltry possession? All I have seen teaches me to trust the Creator for all I have not seen. Whatever it be which the great Providence prepares for us, it must be something large and generous, and in the great style of his works. The future must be up to the style of our faculties, — of memory, of hope, of imagi-

Everything prospective.

Something large and generous.

nation, of reason." "Certainly," quaintly reasons Lord Herbert of Cherbury, "since in my mother's womb this plastica, or formatrix, which formed my eyes, ears, and other senses, did not intend them for that place, but as being conscious of a better life, made them as fitting organs to apprehend and perceive those things which should occur in this world; so I believe, since my coming into this world my soul hath formed or produced certain faculties which are almost as useless for this life as the above-named senses were for the preexisting state: — and these faculties are faith, hope, love, and joy, since they never rest or fix upon any transitory or perishing object in this world, as extending themselves to something further than can be here given, and indeed, acquiesce only in the perfect, eternal, and infinite." "We forget nothing," uttered Thackeray. "The memory sleeps, but wakens again; I often think how it shall be, when, after the last sleep of death, the reveille shall arouse us forever, and the past in one flash of self-consciousness rush back, like the soul, revivified." "God himself," thought Hawthorne, "cannot compensate us for being born for any period short of eternity. All

Reasoning of Lord Herbert.

The reveille after the last sleep.

the misery endured here constitutes a claim for another life, and still more, all the happiness; because all true happiness involves something more than the earth owns, and needs something more than a mortal capacity for the enjoyment of it."

The pendulum of eternity.
Eternity! The pendulum of it! which "beats epochs as ours do seconds." The magnificence of the professor's conception, that if the fixed stars were annihilated we should not be conscious of it for many years, spite of the rapidity with which light travels, gives little idea of duration without end or beginning. "What have we to do with old age?" asks Emerson of Carlyle in one of his letters. "Our existence looks to me more than ever initial. We have come to see the ground and look up materials and tools. The men who have any positive quality are a flying advance party for reconnoitring. We shall yet have a right work, and kings for competitors."

INTUITION AND WORSHIP.
"The impossibility I find myself under of proving there is no God, is a demonstration to me that there is one," is a sentence of La Bruyère. "Consult Zoroaster and Minos and Solon, and the sage Socrates, and the great Cicero; they have all (says

Voltaire) adored a master, a judge, a father: this sublime system is necessary to man; it is the sacred bond of society, the first foundation of holy equity, the curb of the wicked, the hope of the just. If the heavens, despoiled of their augustness, ceased to manifest him; if God did not exist, it would be necessary to invent him. King! if you oppress me, if your majesty disdains the tears of the innocent, my avenger is in the sky: learn to tremble!" Flacourt, in in his History of the Island of Madagascar, gives a sublime prayer, used by the people we call savages: "O Eternal! have mercy upon me, because I am passing away: O Infinite! because I am but a speck: O Most Mighty! because I am weak: O Source of Light! because I draw nigh to the grave: O Omniscient! because I am in darkness: O All-bounteous! because I am poor: O All-sufficient! because I am nothing." Arbousset, a French missionary to South Africa, recounts an extraordinary interview with a Kaffir chief, to whom he was imparting the message of Christianity. "Your tidings," said the wild black man, "are what I want, and I was seeking before I knew you, as you shall hear and judge for yourself. Twelve

[Sidenotes: Adoration necessary to man. A sublime prayer. Interview with a Kaffir chief.]

years ago I went to feed my flock. The weather was hazy. I sat down upon a rock and asked myself sorrowful questions ; yes, sorrowful, because I was unable to answer them. Who has touched the stars with his hands ? The waters are never weary ; they flow from morning till night, from night till morning. Who makes them flow thus ? I cannot see the wind. Who brings it ? Who makes it blow and roar and terrify me ? Do I know how the corn sprouts ? Yesterday there was not a blade in my field ; to-day I returned to the field and found some. Then I buried my face in both my hands." A French scientist passed his childhood in that period of the French Revolution in which religion was proscribed, the churches of his province shut, and sacred words forbidden to be used. "Nevertheless," he says, "I remember that the aspect of the sky made me dream. I always saw in it something that was not of the world. I searched there above for something I did not see, but whose existence I divined. Yes, the intuition of God was within me." "Posterity will perhaps with truth assert," thought Draper, "that Paradise Lost has wrought more intellectual evil than even its base

Asked himself sorrowful questions.

The intuition of God.

contemporaries [the indecent plays of the time], since it has familiarized educated minds with images which, though in one sense sublime, in another are most unworthy, and has taught the public a dreadful materialization of the great and invisible God. A Manichean composition in reality, it was mistaken for a Christian poem." "People treat the divine name," said Goethe, "as if that incomprehensible and most high Being, who is even beyond the reach of thought, were only their equal. If they were impressed by His greatness they would be dumb, and through veneration unwilling to name Him." In the opinion of a great writer, "The time will come when we will not speak of God needlessly but as seldom as possible. We shall not teach dogmatically of his attributes, or dispute concerning his nature. We shall not impose on any one the obligation of prayer, but allow each to worship in the sanctuary of his own conscience. And this will happen when we are truly religious. Then we shall all be so; and the attempt to establish a prescribed religion will be regarded as blasphemy. The love which we bear him will be of an awful nature: prayer will become mysterious,

A Manichean composition.

The sanctuary of conscience.

and the fear of being unworthy will silence the pen of the theologian and the preacher."

FRIEND-SHIP. Friendship is defined by Thoreau as the unspeakable joy and blessing that result to two or more individuals who from constitution sympathize. Such natures are liable to no mistakes, but will know each other through thick and thin. Between two by nature alike and fitted to sympathize there is no veil, and there can be no obstacle. Who are the estranged? Two friends explaining. It is a saying of Apollodorus that when you go to visit a friend at his house, you can perceive his friendliness the moment you enter the door, for first the servant who opens the door looks pleased, then the dog wags its tail and comes up to you, and the first person you meet hands you a chair, before a word has been said. Rowland Hill, on one occasion (preaching to a large congregation on men's trust in the friendship of the world) observed, that his own acquaintances would probably fill the church; and he was quite certain that his friends would only fill the *Born friends.* pulpit. Born friends, said Richter, only find each other a second time, and bring to each other not only a future, but a past also.

In our purblind and crippled state, our IGNORANCE. superstitions and prejudices are our most convenient crutches. The more ignorant we are, the more necessary they seem to us. Poor auxiliaries, we may say, but better than nothing in our many extremities. Something we must have to hold to, as we feel our way in the obscurity of our intelligence and reason; and these poor aids come down to us as a part of the general inheritance of ignorance from the generations that groped before us. Our transgressions are as often blunders as sins. The Japanese do not swear at one another; they say "Fool!" Cave, who was jailer during the two years Hunt was a prisoner, had become a philosopher by the force of his situation. He said to the poet one day, when a new batch of criminals came in, "Poor ignorant wretches, sir!" It is a profound saying of the Chinese, that he who finds pleasure in vice and pain in virtue is a novice in both.

"There's no art to find the mind's con- FACES. struction in the face," though we assume to read it as a book, and to determine from it even the motives of the heart. Quin presumed to say of Macklin's face, painted by Opie, "If God writes a legible hand, that fellow is a villain." Daniel Webster, once when traveling alone in a stage-coach, was in terror of the driver, judging him, from his face, to be a murderer; the driver at the same time was in like dread of the senator, believing him, from his countenance, to be a highwayman. Luttrell said to Moore that often, in speculating on the future fortunes of the young men with whom he lived, he has said to himself, in looking at Wellesley's (Wellington's) vacant face, "Well, let who will get on in this world, you certainly will not." Sir Thomas Lawrence told Barry Cornwall of his having been taken once to visit a female of extreme beauty. A friend of his wished him as an artist to see, and if possible take a study of, this woman. He went accordingly and saw her. She was, he said, most exquisitely beautiful, perhaps more so than any person he had ever seen: but the eye of an artist is quick at detecting faults, and he saw lurking, among her perfections, or rather peeping out from among them occasionally, an expression which was diabolical. He did not like her. Whether he took any sketch or not he did not say; but, he added, that he learned

Wellington's vacant face.

A diabolical expression.

afterwards that "the lady" went to live with a young man, whom she entirely ruined. When in great distress, from her extravagance, she induced him to commit forgery; and when he was taken up for the crime, she appeared and volunteered her evidence against him; and upon her evidence he was hanged. "Portraits of Erasmus are not uncommon; every scholar would know him (says Holmes) in the other world, with the look he wore on earth. All the etchings and their copies give a characteristic presentation of the spiritual precursor of Luther, who pricked the false image with his rapier which the sturdy monk slashed with his broadsword. What a face it is which Hans Holbein has handed down to us in this wonderful portrait at Longford Castle! How dry it is with scholastic labor, how keen with shrewd skepticism, how worldly-wise, how conscious of its owner's wide-awake sagacity! Erasmus and Rabelais, — Nature used up all her arrows for their quivers, and had to wait a hundred years more before she could find shafts enough for the outfit of Voltaire, leaner and keener than Erasmus, and almost as free in his language as the audacious creator of Gargantua and Panta-

Portraits of Erasmus.

Voltaire.

gruel." It has been said that had we no other histories of the Roman emperors but those we find on their money, we should take them for the most virtuous race of princes that mankind were ever blessed with: whereas, if we look into their lives, they appear many of them such monsters of lust and cruelty as are almost a reproach to human nature. Claudius appears as great a conqueror as Julius Cæsar, and Domitian a wiser prince than his brother Titus. Tiberius on his coins is all mercy and moderation, Caligula and Nero are fathers of their country, Galba the pattern of public liberty, and Vitellius the restorer of the city of Rome. In short, if you have a mind to see the religious Commodus, the pious Caracalla, and the devout Heliogabalus, you may find them either in the inscription or device of their medals. One of the poets made a study of the busts of the Roman emperors, and found them, on the whole, interesting. Julius Cæsar heads them, with a face traversed in all directions with wrinkles. He thought he had never beheld such a careworn countenance. Such was the price he paid for ruling his happier fellow-creatures. Nero's face it was sad to contemplate. There is a series of busts of him at different periods of his life: one, that of a charming happy little boy; another, that of a young man, growing uneasy; and a third, that of the miserable tyrant. You fancy that he was thinking of having killed his mother, and was trying to bully his conscience into no care about it. Hogg described Shelley, from appearance, as "a sum of many contradictions." The Duke of Wellington must have found something very interesting in Van Amburgh's face, for he had Landseer paint a picture of the lion-tamer for him. Upon the artist's saying, in reply to the Duke's inquiry, that the price would be six hundred guineas, the Duke wrote out a check for twelve hundred. Lavater says that the character is to be judged not by the expression, which is variable, but by the firm parts and the bony conformation of the countenance. A friend of Emerson's once came upon him while he was sleeping, and was startled at the stern character of a face which he had known only as radiant and inviting. It was a new lesson of the man, which somewhat modified his previous impression. Mr. T. A. Trollope saw much of George Eliot, and was apparently intimate with her, for she once said to him

Bust of Nero, the tyrant.

Lavater's dictum.

in Florence that "she regretted she had been born," an utterance which he attributes entirely to ill-health. His description of her is interesting: "She was not, as the world in general is aware, a handsome, or even a personable woman. Her face was long; the eyes not large nor beautiful in color — they were, I think, of a grayish blue — the hair, which she wore in old-fashioned braids coming low down on either side of her face, of a rather light brown. It was streaked with gray when last I saw her. Her figure was of middle height, large-boned and powerful. It was often said that she inherited from her peasant ancestors a frame and constitution very robust. Her head was finely formed, with a noble and well-balanced arch from brow to crown. The lips and mouth possessed a power of infinitely varied expression. George Lewes once said to me when I made some observation to the effect that she had a sweet face (I meant that the face expressed great sweetness), 'You might say what a sweet hundred faces! I look at her sometimes in amazement. Her countenance is constantly changing.' The said lips and mouth were distinctly sensuous in form and fullness. She has been

George Eliot's face.

Constantly changing.

compared to the portraits of Savonarola (who was frightful) and of Dante (who, though stern and bitter-looking, was handsome). Something there was of both faces in George Eliot's physiognomy. Lewes told us, in her presence, of the exclamation uttered suddenly by some one to whom she was pointed out at a place of public entertainment. 'That,' said a bystander, 'is George Eliot.' The gentleman to whom she was thus indicated gave one swift, searching look, and exclaimed, sotto voce, 'Dante's aunt!'" When Hunt came to England, after an absence of four years abroad, he was grieved at the succession of fair sulky faces which he met in the streets of London. They all appeared to come out of unhappy homes. "Talk of Venus rising from the sea!" exclaimed Douglas Jerrold. "Were I to paint a Venus she should be escaping from a cottage window to join her lover, with a face now white, now red, as the roses nodding about it; an eye like her own star; lips sweetening the jasmine, as it clings to hold them; a face and form in which harmonious thoughts seem as vital breath! Nothing but should speak; her little hand should tell a love-tale; nay, her very foot

Savanarola

"*Dante's aunt.*"

Jerrold's Venus.

planted on the ladder, should utter eloquence enough to stop a hermit at his beads, and make him watchman while the lady fled." The pen-and-ink sketch of Hogarth's which was the only guide of Miss Thomas in modeling the bust of Fielding, not long ago unveiled at Taunton, is the subject of a curious story. Hogarth and Garrick, sitting together in a tavern one day, were lamenting the fact that Fielding had died without a single portrait of him having been taken. "I think," said Garrick, "that I could make his face;" and at once used all his skill as a contortionist to that end. "For Heaven's sake, hold, David!" cried Hogarth; "remain as you are for a few minutes." Garrick did so, and Hogarth sketched the outlines of his face. The portrait was afterward finished according to their mutual recollection, and was the original not only of Miss Thomas's bust, but of every portrait of Fielding now extant. On the wall upstairs, in the private part of a bookseller's establishment in Old Boston, England, there hung (described by Hawthorne) a crayon-portrait of Sterne, never engraved, representing him as a rather young man, blooming, and not uncomely; it was the

Bust of Fielding.

A crayon-portrait of Sterne.

worldly face of a man fond of pleasure, but without that ugly, keen, sarcastic, odd expression that we see in his only engraved portrait. The picture is an original, and must needs be very valuable; and we wish it might be prefixed to some new and worthier biography of a writer whose character the world has always treated with singular harshness, considering how much it was to him. There was likewise a crayon-portrait of Sterne's wife, looking so haughty and unamiable, that the wonder is, not that he ultimately left her, but that he ever contrived to live a week with such an awful woman. George Eliot, in Romola, delineates the face of a traitor. "A perfect traitor," she says, "should have a face which vice can write no marks on — lips that will lie with a dimpled smile — eyes of such agate-like brightness and depth that no infamy can dull them — cheeks that will rise from a murder and not look haggard." It is said that Lamb had a head worthy of Aristotle, with as fine a heart as ever beat in a human bosom, and limbs very fragile to sustain it. There was a caricature of him sold in the shops, which pretended to be a likeness. Procter went into the shop in a passion, and asked the

Portrait of Sterne's wife.

Lamb's head.

man what he meant by putting forth such a libel. The man apologized, and said that the artist meant no offense. There never was a true portrait of Lamb. In that wonderful picture of Leonardo, The Last Supper, it is fancied that the heads of the Apostles are from the men of his own time, but the face of the Lord, by a perfect study of chiaroscuro, radiates the light upon the groups, and claims the principal admiration of the beholder. There is a story that the artist, having finished the rest, could not paint this; he found it one morning miraculously finished.

<small>*No true portrait of Lamb.*</small>

<small>HEREDITY.</small> The law of heredity is more and more being recognized, investigated, and regarded. The body, more and more, is being esteemed the tabernacle of a soul, and an added sacredness attached to it accordingly. "There is but one temple in the world," says Novalis, "and that temple is the body of man. Nothing is holier than this high form. Bending before men is a reverence done to this revelation in the flesh. We touch Heaven, when we lay our hands on a human body." There is a song made in honor of Allan, the famous captain of Clanranald, who fell at Sherrif-muir.

His servant, who lay on the field watching his master's dead body, being asked next day, who that was, answered, "He was a man yesterday." The grandson of Mahomet was slain with three and thirty strokes of lances and swords. After they had trampled on his body, they carried his head to the castle of Cufa, and the inhuman governor struck him on the mouth with a cane. "Alas!" exclaimed an aged Mussulman, "on these lips have I seen the lips of the apostle of God!" Johnson asked one of his executors, a few days before his death, "Where do you intend to bury me?" He answered, "In Westminster Abbey." "Then," continued Johnson, "if my friends think it worth while to give me a stone, let it be placed over me so as to protect me." "Bless not thyself only," says the great Sir Thomas Browne, in Religio Medici, "that thou wast born in Athens; but, among thy multiplied acknowledgments, lift up one hand to heaven, that thou wert born of honest parents, that modesty, humility, and veracity, lay in the same egg, and came into the world with thee. From such foundations thou mayest be happy in a virtuous precocity, and make an early and long walk in goodness; so mayest thou

The grandson of Mahomet.

Johnson's request.

more naturally feel the contrariety of vice unto nature, and resist some by the antidote of thy temper." Dr. Young writes of "That hideous sight, a naked human heart." "I saw," says Leigh Hunt, "a worse sight than the heart, in a journey which I took in a neighboring county. It was an infant, all over sores, and cased in steel; the result of the irregularities of its father; and I confess that I would rather have seen the heart of the very father of that child, than I would the child himself. I am sure it must have bled at the sight. I am sure there would have been a feeling of some sort to vindicate nature, granting that up to that moment the man had been a fool or even a scoundrel." An eminent writer upon Responsibility in Mental Disease remarks, "When one considers the reckless way in which persons, whatever the defects of their mental and bodily constitution, often get married, without sense of responsibility for the miseries which they entail upon those who will be the heirs of their infirmities, without regard, in fact, to anything but their own present gratification, one is driven to think either that man is not the preëminently reasoning and moral animal which he claims to

A hideous sight.

Reckless marriage.

be, or that there is in him an instinct which is deeper than knowledge. He has persuaded himself, rightly or wrongly, that in this case there is in the feeling of love between the sexes something of so sacred and mysterious a character as to justify disregard to consequences in marriage. *Consequences.* We have only to look at the large part which love fills in novels, poetry, and painting; and to consider what a justification of unreason in life it is held to be, to realize what a hold it has on him in his present state of development, and what a repugnance there would be to quench its glow by cold words of reason. At bottom, however, there is nothing particularly holy about it; on the contrary, it is a passion which man shares with other animals; and when its essential nature and function are regarded, we shall nowhere find stronger evidence of a community of nature between man and animals. It would not be a very absurd thing if an ingenious person, considering curiously what a solemn undertaking marriage is, and what serious responsibilities it entails, were to maintain that men and women should enter into it soberly and rather sadly, under a grave sense of responsibility, as upon an un- *A solemn undertaking.*

Rejoicings should be reserved.

certain voyage, and should reserve their rejoicings for the journey's end, when, having acted well their parts, they might fairly claim a nunc plaudite." "If you have seen the picture-gallery of any one old family," says Dickens in The Old Curiosity Shop, "you will remember how the same face and figure — often the fairest and slightest of them all — come upon you in different generations; and how you trace the same sweet girl through a long line of portraits — never growing old or changing — the Good Angel of the race — abiding by them in all reverses — redeeming all their sins."

Education a sum of habits.

Education, in the opinion of Ribot, is a sum of habits. "Compare," he says, "the savage with the accomplished gentleman, and how great is the difference. The fact is that six thousand years and more stand between the two. Many of the habits which we contract through education have cost the race centuries of effort. Education has to fix in us the results achieved by hundreds of generations. Millions of men have been needed to invent and bring to perfection those methods which develop the body, cultivate the mind, and fashion the manners. We are sometimes amazed at seeing nations highly civilized, gentle, humane, charitable in time of peace, giving themselves up to every excess as soon as war has broken out. The reason of this is that war, being a return to the savage state, awakens the primitive nature of man, as it subsisted prior to culture, and brings it back with all its heroic daring, its worship of force, and its boundless lusts. In China, when a man has committed a capital crime, a minute inquiry is first made into his physical condition, his temperament, his mental complexion, his prior acts; nor does the investigation stop at the individual — it is concerned with the most inconsiderable antecedents of the members of his family, and is even carried back to his ancestry. In the case of high treason, or when a prince is assassinated, the Chinese prescribe 'that the culprit shall be cut up into ten thousand pieces, and that his sons and grandsons shall be put to death.'" In Darwin's Expression of the Emotions in Man and Animals, there is an authentic account of a habit occurring in individuals of three consecutive generations. It was, when each lay fast asleep on his back in bed, of raising his right arm slowly in front of his face, up to his forehead, and then dropping it with a jerk, so that the wrist

What war awakens.

Sons and grandsons put to death.

fell heavily on the bridge of his nose. The trick did not occur every night, but occasionally, and was independent of any ascertained cause. Rabelais felt sure that he must have been the son of a king, because nobody had more princely inclinations. "We incline in the same manner," says the author of Wishing-Cap Papers, "to be so young in our feelings, and to desire such a good long life before us to do a world of things in, that it seems as if we had a right to it. Mortality is a good provision, considering that the world has not come to its state of enjoyment, and that people in general, by the time they are forty, hardly know what to do with their Sundays; but an exception might be made, we think, in favor of those who could occupy all their hours some way or other a hundred years to come, and who have not yet got over their love even of gingerbread." "If by the visitation of God," writes Holmes in his remarkable Elsie Venner, "a person receives any injury which impairs the intellect or the moral perceptions, is it not monstrous to judge such a person by our common working standards of right and wrong? Certainly, everybody will answer, in cases where there is a palpable organic change brought about, as when a blow on the head produces insanity. Fools! How long will it be before we shall learn that for every wound which betrays itself to the sight by a scar, there are a thousand unseen mutilations that cripple, each of them, some one or more of our highest faculties." The same author in his Mechanism in Thought and Morals, expresses the view that "When we can take the dimensions of virtue by triangulation; when we can literally weigh Justice in her own scales; when we can speak of the specific gravity of truth, or the square root of honesty; when we can send a statesman his integrity in a package to Washington, if he happen to have left it behind — then we may begin to speak of the moral character of inherited tendencies, which belong to the machinery on which the Sovereign Power alone is responsible. The misfortune of perverse instincts, which adhere to us as congenital inheritances, should go to our side of the account, if the books of heaven are to be kept as the great Church of Christendom maintains they are, by double entry."

A thousand unseen mutilations.

Moral character of inherited tendencies.

THE LACONIC. Joubert had a habit, from his twentieth year to his seventieth, of jotting down with a pencil the best issues of his meditation as they arose, and out of this chaos of notes was shaped, many years after his death, a full volume of Thoughts. "If there be a man," he said, "plagued with the accursed ambition of putting a whole volume into a page, a whole page into a sentence, and that sentence into a word, it is I." *Farquhar.* When Farquhar was near the end of his gay yet checkered career, death, the glory of his last success, and the thought of his children, pressing hard upon him, he wrote this laconic, but perfectly intelligible, note to Wilks: "Dear Bob, — I have not anything to leave thee, to perpetuate my memory, but two helpless girls; look upon them sometimes, and think of him that was, to the last moment of his life, — George Farquhar." Farquhar's confidence in his friend was like that of La Fontaine, *La Fontaine.* who, having lost a home, was met in the street by a friend who invited him to his. "I was going there," said the simple-minded poet. Wilks did not disappoint Farquhar's expectations. Quin had withdrawn to Bath. Garrick's triumphs had soured him. He desired to be asked back to Covent Garden, but Rich would not humor him. The one wrote, "I am at Bath; yours, James Quin": and the other answered, "Stay there, and be d——; yours, John Rich." W. H. Crawford, Secretary of the Treasury, wrote to S. Dinsmore, collector at the port of Mobile: "Treasury Department, Washington, Jan. 15, 1822. Sir: This Department is desirous of knowing how far the Tombigbee river runs up. You will please communicate the information. Respectfully. W. H. Crawford. S. Dinsmore, Esq., collector, Mobile." "Mobile, Feb'y 7th, 1822. Sir: I have the honor to acknowledge the receipt of your letter of the 15th ult., and of informing you, in reply, that the Tombigbee does not run up at all. S. Dinsmore. Hon. W. H. Crawford, Secretary of the Treasury." "Treasury Department, Washington, March 1st, 1822. Sir: I have the honor to inform you that this Department has no further services for you as Collector of Mobile. Respectfully. W. H. Crawford. S. Dinsmore, Mobile." Dr. Franklin wrote to Strahan: "Philadelphia, July 5, 1775. Mr. Strahan: You are a member of that parliament, and have formed a part of that majority, which has condemned my native

Official.

Franklin to Strahan.

country to destruction. You have begun to burn our towns, and to destroy their inhabitants. Look at your hands, — they are stained with the blood of your relations and your acquaintances. You and I were long friends; you are at present my enemy, and I am, Yours, B. Franklin."

Countess of Dorset. The Countess of Dorset replied to Sir Joseph Williamson, secretary of state to Charles II., nominating to her a member for the borough of Appleby: "I have been bullied by an usurper, I have been neglected by a court, but I will not be dictated to by a subject — your man shan't stand." Sir

Sir Philip Sidney. Philip Sidney wrote to the secretary of his father as lord deputy: "Mr. Molineaux: Few words are best. My letters to my father have come to the eyes of some. Neither can I condemn any but you for it. If it be so, you have played the very knave with me; and so I will make you know, if I have good proof of it. But that for so much as is past. For that is to come, I assure you before God, that if I ever know you to do so much as read any letter I write to my father, without his commandment, or my consent, I will thrust my dagger into you. And trust to it, for I speak it in earnest. In the mean time farewell. From Court, this last of May, 1578. By me, Philip Sidney." Rufus Choate and Daniel Webster were once opposed to each other as lawyers in a suit which turned on the size of certain wheels. Mr. Choate filled the air with the rockets of rhetoric, and dazzled the jury, but Mr. Webster caused the wheels to be brought into court and put behind a screen. When he rose to speak the screen was removed, and his only reply to Choate's eloquence was, "Gentlemen! there are the wheels!" A spy named Palmer, sent by Sir Henry Clinton, the British commander, had been detected furtively collecting information of the force and condition of the post at Peekskill, and had undergone a military trial. A vessel of war came up the Hudson in all haste, and landed a flag of truce at Verplanck's Point, by which a message was transmitted to Putnam from Clinton claiming the said Palmer as a lieutenant in the British service. Putnam replied: "Head-Quarters, 7th August, 1777. Edward Palmer, an officer in the enemy's service, was taken as a spy lurking within our lines; he has been tried as a spy, and shall be executed as a spy; and the flag is ordered to depart immediately. Israel Putnam.

Choate and Webster.

Putnam to Clinton.

P. S. He has, accordingly, been executed."
A young lady having gone out to India, and
writing home to her friends, concluded:

An important postscript. "P. S. You will see by my signature that I
am married." An answer to the Bishop of
Norwich, in acknowledgment of an invitation, is reported: "Mr. O.'s private affairs
turn out so sadly that he cannot have the
pleasure of waiting upon his lordship at his
agreeable home on Monday next. N. B.
His wife is dead." Foote's mother had
been heiress to a large fortune, spent it all,
and was at length imprisoned for debt. In

Foote and his mother. this condition she wrote to Sam, who had
been allowing her a hundred a year out of
the proceeds of his acting, "Dear Sam, I
am in prison for debt; come and assist
your loving mother, E. Foote." Sam replied, "Dear Mother, so am I, which prevents his duty being paid to his loving
mother by her affectionate son, Sam Foote."

Voltaire and Piron. "Eo rus," wrote Voltaire one day, to notify
Piron that he was "going into the country"; Piron, to surpass this epistle in
brevity, replied by one letter, "I," which
is Latin for "go." "Will you breakfast
with me to-morrow? S. R.," was Rogers'
invitation to a celebrated wit and beauty.
"Won't I? H. D.," was the response.

"My Dear Dorset, I have just been married, and am the happiest dog alive. (Signed) Berkeley." Answer: "My Dear Berkeley, Every dog has his day. (Signed) Dorset." A young man at college addressed his uncle: "My Dear Uncle — Ready for the needful. Your affectionate Nephew." To which the uncle replied: "My Dear Nephew — The needful is not ready. Your affectionate Uncle." John Randolph sometimes met his match, as in a contest on one occasion on the floor of the House of Representatives with Daniel Sheffey, a Virginian, who had risen by the force of his talents from the humble position of shoemaker. "Let the cobbler stick to his last," said Randolph, in scornful allusion to Sheffey's former occupation. "If the gentleman had been raised a cobbler he would be a cobbler now," was the splendid retort. It was, we believe, the eminent Tristam Burges, of Rhode Island, who made even a better reply to the caustic Virginian. They were standing together on the steps of the Capitol when a drove of mules passed by. "Some of your constituents," said Randolph, pointing to the long line of long-eared quadrupeds. "Yes," responded Burges; "going South to teach school."

Uncle and nephew.

Randolph.

Burges.

MONOTONY AND FAMILIARITY.

"The monotonous don't interest me any longer," said a pretty young woman who waited upon Dr. Bellows and his party at the Schangli, the most commanding prospect of the Bernese Alps, as she witnessed their enthusiasm when the setting sun had set the whole chain into a flame of beauty. She had seen too much of them. "All the world comes here to see these mountains," said an interesting peasant girl at the opening of the valley of Chamouni, "and I wish they would carry Mont Blanc away with them — a great snow-bank, spoiling our harvests in autumn, and carrying away our bridges in spring, and killing our husbands and brothers who have to climb it for you strangers, so curious about such a common thing. Everybody wants to come here, and I only want to get away. I am saving all the money I can get to go to Geneva, and perhaps to Paris." The agents of the Hudson Bay Company are

Barrack life. described as leading their barrack life by rule, sitting down at stated hours to the same primitive fare, in the company that has become only too familiar. They must have "sucked each other's brains" till the exhaustion is complete, and traveled over every inch of their respective minds till they know them as well as the bit of prairie that lies round their stockade. It was the opinion of Hazlitt that in the course of a long acquaintance we have repeated all our good things, and discussed all our favorite topics several times over, so that our conversation becomes a mockery of social intercourse. We might as well talk to ourselves. The soil of friendship is worn out with constant use. Habit may still attach us to each other, but we feel ourselves fettered by it. Old friends might be compared to old married people without the tie of children. It may seem a hard and worldly thing to say, says the author of The Intellectual Life, but it appears to me that a wise man might limit his intercourse with others before there was any danger of satiety, as it is wisdom in eating to rise from table with an appetite. Certainly, if the friends of our intellect live near enough for us to anticipate no permanent separation from them by mere distance, if we may expect to meet them frequently, to have many opportunities for a more thorough and searching exploration of their minds, it is a wise policy not to exhaust them all at once.

An opinion of Hazlitt's.

Danger of satiety.

Vauvenargues, in one of his Maxims, defines indolence to be the sleep of the mind. You remember the vivid picture of Dickens', describing Gabriel Varden, standing working at his anvil, his face all radiant with exercise and gladness, his sleeves turned up, his wig pushed off his shining forehead — the easiest, freest, happiest man in all the world. Beside him sat a sleek cat, purring and winking in the light, and falling every now and then into an idle doze, as from excess of comfort. You remember also the twenty-fourth stanza of Thomson's Castle of Indolence — the laziest lines in literature: —

SLEEP OF THE MIND.

Excess of comfort.

> "Waked by the crowd, slow from his bench arose
> A comely, full-fed porter, swoln with sleep:
> His calm, broad, thoughtless aspect breathed repose;
> And in sweet torpor he was plungèd deep,
> Ne could himself from ceaseless yawning keep;
> While o'er his eyes the drowsy liquor ran,
> Through which his half-waked soul would faintly peep:
> Then taking his black staff, he called his man,
> And roused himself as much as rouse himself he can."

Agassiz's sloth.

Agassiz, in his Journey to Brazil, speaks of a sloth on board his vessel on the Amazon, — the most fascinating of all his pets — not for his charms, but for his oddities. "I am never tired," he says, "of watching him, he looks so deliciously lazy. His head sunk in his arms, his whole attitude lax and indifferent, he seems to ask only for rest. If you push him, or if, as often happens, a passer-by gives him a smart tap to arouse him, he lifts his head and drops his arms so slowly, so deliberately, that they hardly seem to move, raises his heavy lids and lets his large eyes rest upon your face for a moment with appealing, hopeless indolence; then the lids fall softly, the head droops, the arms fold heavily about it, and he collapses again into absolute repose." This mute remonstrance was the nearest approach to activity the naturalist saw him make. Lamb, in his delicious essay On Some of the Old Actors, says of Dodd, that "in expressing slowness of apprehension he surpassed all others. You could see the first dawn of an idea stealing slowly over his countenance, climbing up by little and little, with a painful process, till it closed up at last to the fullness of a twilight conception — its highest meridian. He seemed to keep back his intellect, as some have had the power to retard their pulsation. The balloon takes less time in filling, than it took to cover the expansion of his broad moony face over all its quarters with expression. A glimmer of understanding would appear in the corner of his eye, and for lack of fuel go out again. A part of his forehead would catch a little intelligence, and be a long time in communicating it to the remainder." One day, at the one store of a cross-roads village, I had convenient means of witnessing a scene which has remained in my memory. It was in summer, and the laziest day of the season. Waiting for a friend, I had ample opportunity to observe an interesting person who sat a few feet from me. He was evidently in perfect health, and perfectly at his ease in his life and possessions. His complexion and figure were proof of unconscious digestion, undisturbed circulation, and absolute repose of nerves. Everything about him, indeed, denoted an utter absence of sensation. He was a farmer, there was no doubt — in full enjoyment of enough of earth's fat acres, and a generous sufficiency of all fat things. There were no burdens or cumbersome improvements on his land, and he was happy in the possession of it.

At a cross-roads village.

An utter absence of sensation.

> "Wi' sma' to sell, and less to buy,
> Aboon distress, below envy,
> Oh who wad leave this humble state,
> For a' the pride of a' the great?"

He had come over to the neighborhood store to buy something, and had sat him down with the newspaper, at the open door, in the sweet air, to read; but he was too comfortable, or the task was too great — he had made no progress. The paper had slipped from him, and his hand had the expression of reaching for it, but the will was wanting to move it. He was not, as we say, asleep, but only profoundly reposing — dreaming, as his faculties would permit — drowned, as they were, in excess of comfort — deep down in the still depths of tranquillity, where the mind rests — free of currents, friction, or fretting. His eyes were nearly closed, as if to remain so. He seemed to be absolutely unconscious of the little life that was about him. A boy, passing before him, made no more impression than the shadow of a cloud. An express train rushed by, a few rods from where he sat: the newspaper felt it, and moved — the man not at all. Animated conversation sprang up; spirit and humor prevailed. A story was told. The newspaper moved again a little; at last, the man. His mind slowly waked from its blissful state; eyelids lifted; eyes brightened; sides shook; and a burst of laugh-

At the open door, in the sweet air.

The newspaper moved — the man not at all.

ter was heard — showing, not only appreciation, but thankfulness, that another enjoyment had been reserved for him, to fill up his cup of happiness to boundless overflowing.

<small>THE FRIENDLY GUIDANCE OF NECESSITY.</small>

It is a true saying, that opportunity is kind, but only to the industrious. The Persians have a legend that a poor man watched a thousand years before the gate of Paradise. Then, when he snatched one little nap, — it opened, and shut. Dr. John, in Villette, throughout his whole life, was a man of luck — a man of success. And why? Because he had the eye to see his opportunity, the heart to prompt to well-timed action, the nerve to consummate a perfect work. And no tyrant-passion dragged him back; no enthusiasms, no foibles encumbered his way. "To win," said von Moltke, "you must be at the right place at the right time with a superior force." A distinguished traveler was struck with the excess of wealth and luxury in the old countries, where persons of original or splendid gifts are obliged to invent careers for themselves, being denied the friendly guidance of necessity. When Sir Horace Vere died, it was asked what had

<small>A saying of von Moltke's.</small>

occasioned his death; to which some one replied, "By doing nothing." Among the companions of Reynolds, when he was studying his art at Rome, was a fellow-pupil of the name of Astley. They made an excursion, with some others, on a sultry day, and all except Astley took off their coats. After some taunts he was persuaded to do the same, and displayed on the back of his waistcoat a foaming waterfall. Necessity had compelled him to patch his clothes with one of his own landscapes. Montesquieu, alluding in a letter to one of his works, says to his correspondent, "You will read it in a few hours, but the labor expended upon it has whitened my hair." Fortune, it has been said, does not like a swordsman, she scorns to encounter a fearful man: there is no honor in the victory where there is no danger in the way to it; she tries Mencius by fire; Rutilius by exile; Socrates by poison; Cato by death. It is only in adverse fortune, and in bad times, that we find great examples.

A fellow-pupil of Reynolds'

The Orientals, as clearly stated, defined Fate to be the penalty of deeds committed in a former state of existence. And the like penalty is reaffirmed by Jews and

THE PALM OF DESTINY

Christians, ancestral sins being visited upon the children even to the third and fourth generation, — by imputation upon the race itself. "Fate is a hand," say the Orientals. "It lays two fingers on the eyes, two on the ears, one on the mouth, and ever cries, Be still." Fate, the philosophers define to be, "a name for facts not yet passed under the fire of thought; — for causes which are unpenetrated." Materialists give it the name of destiny. "I do not," said Carlyle, "quake in my bed like Wordsworth, trying to reconcile the ways of Providence to my apprehension. I early came to the conclusion that I was not very likely to make it out clearly: the notions of the Calvinists seem what you cannot escape from, namely, that if it's all known beforehand, why, it all must happen." It is now twenty years ago or more since a morning's walk led me by Bellevue Hospital and the Morgue. It was on Sunday, and in dog-days — the close of a heated term. The temperature was high in the eighties, and steadily rising. I saw, as I crossed over one of the street railroads, that the iron rails had already expanded to an extent to bow them perceptibly. Crossing the avenue to the hospital corner, I

particularly noticed the people going in
and coming out of the dead-house, and that *The dead-house.*
they emerged with very different counte-
nances than they went in with. Generally
a sort of social exchange, it was evident
that on this occasion, for some reason, it
was a serious place, discouraging to socia-
bility. Persons that went in together chatting, came out apart, and with grave faces.
Curiosity, which in great part had led them *Curiosity confounded.*
thither, was confounded, and a bitter lesson
of life had been impressed on their minds.
I passed by. The smell of salt water at
the foot of the street, as it lapped the piles
and timbers, made me linger, though compelled to listen to the yelping and snarling
and fighting of the dogs at the pound hard
by. The peculiar types of men the canine
unfortunates brought about them were of
interest, and to an extent diverted my attention from the miserable noises. Opposite the Morgue I lingered again, and again
noticed the marked differences of expres- *Differences of expres-*
sion upon faces as they went in and came *sion.*
out. Never having visited a place of the
sort, and never having had a desire to do
so, on this occasion I felt an irresistible inclination to cross over. I did so, and went
in. The mystery of the changed faces was

soon enough explained. Three or more of the marble slabs within the glass-inclosed room were occupied by dead bodies, — two of which immediately engaged my attention. They lay side by side, covered to the neck with rubber cloth, streams of water from pipes above breaking over them and running away at the edges. Two poor dead human bodies could hardly have been more different in appearance. They were women, and apparently of about the same age. One had light, soft hair, and a very fair, delicate complexion; the face in every feature was remarkably beautiful; the eyelids, not entirely closed, revealed a line of bright blue under the long lashes; the forehead of breadth and height and expression to denote unusual cultivation; the delicate ears almost transparent; the nose straight, with nostrils exquisitely thin and sensitive; the mouth of peculiar refinement and sweetness; lips not wholly covering rows of perfectly white teeth; chin and cheeks with dimples still in them; throat and neck shapely enough to suggest happy achievements to sculpture; — looking, altogether, like the face of opulence, — the face of a bright human being who just now was the centre of intelligence and elegance — the

Two poor dead human bodies.

Face of opulence.

petted favorite of enlightenment and the social virtues. She looked to be the descendant of long lines of gentlemen and ladies, whose faces had been set against evil, and whose aspirations were upward and pure — the best fruit of the best and most encouraging civilization. The other unfortunate was of a totally different type. Her complexion was cloudy and forbidding; her hair black and coarse; her brow low and marked by lines of distress; her cheek-bones high, and jaws square and set, as if in habitual desperate resistance to fate; eyes close shut and shrunken; two ugly scars, one on the forehead and the other behind one of her ears, disfigured and marked her as a victim of grossness and brutality. The head and face were expressive of degradation and wretchedness, and remain to me to this day a haunting memory. Alas the life too plainly written in the hard lines and sinewy conformation. Existence had been a struggle — life an unequal and awful battle. She had suffered the ills of generations. Her father and her grandfather likely had been anything but gentlemen; her mother and grandmother anything but ladies. Poor unfortunates! Side by side they lay, skimmed

The other of a different type.

Life an unequal and awful battle.

off the bay the same hour. Through what devious and diverse ways they had met in this horrible place. Human nature and human·experience stand dumb in the presence of such facts of life. The inevitable, the irremediable — who can even guess to what extent? — had to all appearance determined the end of these two poor human creatures. Call it fate, call it destiny, call it predestination, — in effect it is the same; all philosophies and all religions to a greater or less extent include it, and we all unconsciously bow to it.

Dumb in the presence of such facts of life.

"What has God given to the wren? Content." St. Jenny (created and canonized by Jerrold) was wedded to a very poor man; they had scarcely bread to keep them; but Jenny was of so sweet a temper that even want bore a bright face, and Jenny always smiled. In the worst seasons Jenny would spare crumbs for the birds, and sugar for the bees. Now it so happened that one autumn a storm rent their cot in twenty places apart; when, behold, between the joints, from the basement to the roof, there was nothing but honeycomb and honey — a little fortune for St. Jenny and her husband, in honey.

CONTENT.

A little fortune in honey.

Now, some one said it was the bees, but more declared it was the sweet temper and contentment of St. Jenny that had filled the poor man's house with honey. When Pittacus, after the death of his brother, who had left him a good estate, was offered a great sum of money by the king of Lydia, he thanked him for his kindness, but told him he had already more by half than he knew what to do with. In short, content is equivalent to wealth, and luxury to poverty; or, to give the thought a more agreeable turn, "Content is natural wealth," says Socrates; to which Addison adds, "Luxury is artificial poverty;" and recommends to the consideration of those who are always aiming after superfluous and imaginary enjoyments, and will not be at the trouble of contracting their desires, an excellent saying of Bion the philosopher; namely, that "No man has so much care as he who endeavors after the most happiness." "After all," wrote Bulwer to Lady Blessington, "a very little could suffice to make us happy, were it not for our own desires to be happier still. Certainly I think, as we grow older, we grow more cheerful; externals please us more; and were it not for those dead passions which we call

Content equivalent to wealth.

Bulwer to Lady Blessington.

memories, and which have ghosts no exorcism can lay, we might walk on soberly to the future, and dispense with excitement by the way. If we cannot stop Time, it is something to shoe him with felt, and prevent his steps from creaking."

<small>DEMOCRACY.</small>
It would seem that in the United States of America all things promising are to be tried. Societies are to be organized for everything, corporations multiplied indefinitely, and legislation exhausted to make and to keep everybody honest, temperate, and virtuous. Both sexes and all colors are to be educated together. Suffrage is to be universal. Distinctions of God are to be unrecognized by men. An ideal government of the people, it is to know no distinctions, and permit none. Nothing shall be impossible to it. Whimsical at times it will appear, but its whimsicalities will be the recreations and gambols of power. So generally and intensely preoccupied, it is but natural that sometimes a child should <small>Its favoritism fickle and qualified.</small> lead it. Its favoritism, more and more, will be fickle and qualified. More and more it will delight to scatter its gifts, limiting their tenure to subordination. Individuals may be its favorites, until they assume to

be, when they are not. The rights it would secure to each are not to be incompatible with the rights of any. Opportunity for all, advantages to none. All elements must come under control, and be compounded. Masses it will ostentatiously affect, not individuals. Heads so much on a level, one above the rest will be an obstruction. If a quiet blow will reduce it, down it must go. "To live alone is the chastisement of whoever will raise himself too high." Kings have no company. What one knows all will be understood to know. Weaknesses and interests will be accommodated. What affects one must affect all. The materialities — where the attempt is made to make all things material — will increasingly govern. Wealth, more and more, will be — acknowledged or not — the omnipotent distinction. Society at large, accustomed to its aggressive splendor and monopoly of advantages, will bow down to it, envy it, and hate it unconsciously — unconscious all the time of its own growing enslavement. Intellect and purity — come to be regarded as the creations of the schoolmaster and the legislator — will submit to be graded, averaged, and appropriated — kneaded, so to speak, by the

Masses it will ostentatiously affect.

Wealth the omnipotent distinction.

hand of the master — without resistance or sense of responsibility — till the end comes. A scrupulously applied Christianity, purifying, protecting, and directing the ballot, and reducing the universal selfishness to its minimum, must of course dissolve all that is gloomy or discouraging in any outlook, speculation, or conjecture.

<small>PROUD POSSESSORS.</small> Michelet describes a French peasant on a Sunday morning, walking out in his clean linen and unsoiled blouse. His wife is at church, and this simple farmer paces across his acres and looks fondly at his land. You see him in solitude, but his face is illuminated when he thinks his farm is his own, from the surface of the globe to its centre, and that the climate is his own from the surface of the earth up to the seventh heaven. You find that man, if a stranger approaches him, withdrawing, that he may enjoy his affection in soli- <small>*The French peasant's Sunday walk.*</small> tude; and as he turns away from his Sunday walk through his own pastures, you notice that he looks back over his shoulder with affection, and parts with regret. He is not at work; he is not out to keep off interlopers; he is out simply to enjoy the feeling of ownership and to look upon him-

self as a member of responsible society. The cit also is proudly at his ease, and paces the avenue a sovereign in his possessions. What to him are acres and plowshares compared with the great town of which he is a part? The vast congeries of activities and forces exists and is operated for his convenience and comfort. Plans he could not originate are ready made. The flow of his life is in a common channel. The full volume and steady current satisfy his efforts, and the chances of movement float him momentarily to the top. Happy or wretched, he can touch a thousand like him. The best and worst of everything are at hand, and contiguous. The virtues and vices are organized, and recruiting. The great town is the greatest, and he is a part of it. Helping to make it, he does something, and will not have lived in vain. He does not see how, but he would be missed. He expands with the bigness about him. The great assemblage makes him decorous. His conduct disgraces or dignifies it. He dresses to be presentable to it. It keeps a guard over him while he sleeps and knows his footsteps when awake. The streets are lit for him. The parks are planted for him. The harbor is

The cit also proudly at his ease.

Expands with the bigness about him.

The harbor broader for his eye. broader for his eye. An opera he may hear at the Academy for a guinea, or at the cathedral for a shilling. Church privileges are purchasable or acceptable, at will. The cemetery, where they bury in tombs and trenches, is one of his possessions. All are his as much as anybody's, and his without exciting anybody's envy or cupidity. Each illustrates the fable of the swimming apples, and applies it to the rest. The universal hat is lifted in condescension and recognition.

RESPONSIBILITY. If we truly believed and realized that here we begin to be what we are to be ever, how absorbing and responsible life would be. How conscientiously and persistently we should seek the good and avoid the evil. How carefully we should guard ourselves against whatever must perish with the body, and how ardently cultivate all which must survive it. Happiness would not be sought in its transient forms. Life would be appreciated by its *The duty of the hour the duty of all time.* resultant uses. The duty of the hour would be the duty of all time. The good would inhere. The present would be realized as the period of growth and achievement; and having something to do worth doing, we should need all the time we have to do it well. The duties of the day faithfully discharged, we should not much concern ourselves about the morrow. The morrow would be so far provided for that it would be anticipated and made easy, if it come. Refinement and intelligence and excellence would result from fidelity to duty, and a happiness would be established as serene as it would be unconscious. Living and acting, and getting the pleasure and good of life with each day of it, we should enjoy a foretaste of fruition and perpetuity.

The morrow anticipated and made easy.

[Titles for essays, with some citations and hints.]

ESSAYS IN TITLES.

Malignant Joy. — Edmund Kean's acting.

Monopolists of Salvation.

The Heroism of Self-Denial.

Indolence and Cowardice.— At the bottom of too many of our beliefs and practices.

Pitiers of Themselves. — Emerson.

Doubt. — De Tocqueville's three miseries.

Pride and Conscience. — Poe's Marginalia.

"My Dear Devil." — The fidelity of woman.

Dodging the Drops.

Organic Egotism.

An Embodiment of Nothing.

Animal Spirits. — "My distresses are so many that I can't afford to part with my spirits."

The Difficult Ways of Honesty.

Life, the Touchstone of Profession.

One-Eyed Men. — "It is only in the kingdom of the blind that one-eyed men are kings."

Sally Jackson's Dream-Book.

Faith in Knavery. — Jonas Chuzzlewit.

The Books That Have Flavor.

The Fidelity of Silence.

Avarice of Reward.

Keyholes. — Tom Jones.

Milk and Praise. — Mary Lamb.

Morbid Oblivion. — Johnson to Boswell.

Medicines for the Mind. — A saying of Burke's. Holmes in the Autocrat. Burns. Old pamphlet of Dr. Wayland's.

Summer Friends. — Timon of Athens.

Falsehood of Extremes. — Justice without mercy.

An Autumnal Harvest of Leisure. — Wordsworth's letter to Crabb Robinson.

Sensibility of Reproach.—Swift. Steele's last paper of the Englishman.

The Dismal Precocity of Poverty. — Becky Sharp.

Intellectual Detachment.

Sour Bread. — Hawthorne's great horror. Marble Faun.

The Brutality of Justice. — To be treated satirically.

The Sniveling Virtue of Meekness. — Walter Shandy.

Incorrigible and Losing Honesty. — Lamb's father.

Ornamental Sorrow. — The Widow Rowens.

A Habit of Virtue. — Sterne.

Constitutional Inertness.

Ferocious Discontent.

The Dull Virtuous and the Brilliant Wicked.

A Glutton of Books.

Solemn Plausibilities.

Avarice in Youth.

Protracted Misery.

Expansive Intentions. — Skimpole.

Snappishness of Tone. — The brisk old.

Domestic Dyspepsia. — The name given to the disease of which Jane Carlyle was a chronic sufferer, by Caroline Fox.

The Decencies of Ignorance. — John Buncle.

Too Quickly Won. — Romeo and Juliet.

The Holy Goggle. — Halifax's advice to his daughter.

The Infirmity of Pride. — Bulwer's Earl of Warwick.

Other People's Sins.

The Equity of Providence. — Rasselas.

Microscopic Eyes.

Socrates' Sauce.

Foresight of Troubles. — John Buncle.

Unfinished Faces.

The Devil's Amanuensis. — A misanthropic writer. Hazlitt's Commonplaces. Humboldt. Schopenhauer. Sir Thomas Browne.

Aggressive Self-Possession.

The Rapture of Ravage.

Cork John. — Nimble. Always atop.

The Infinite Malice of Destiny. — Shelley to Hogg.

Omnigenous Erudition. — Celestial Railroad.

The Feeling of Identity and the Instinct of Perpetuity.

Married Misery.

The Wild Thunder Months. — Richter.

Disenchanted Maturity. — "The years

that bring the philosophic mind." Prelude to Laon and Cythna.

Patent Antifrictions. — Oil of flattery, etc.

The Air of Omnipotence.

Moral Physicians.

Wise Slowness. — Sainte-Beuve. Mad. Geoffrin.

Raking the Desk of the Devil. — Byron's club-foot. Byron and his sister. Napoleon and his sisters. Memoirs of Mad. de Rémusat.

The Medicine of Example.

The Healing Power of Admiration.

The Etiquette of Sectarianism. — George Eliot.

Running a Thought to Death.

The Popularity-Hunting Air.

Post Mortem Wisdom.

The Habit of Belief.

The Diseases of Sorrow.

Suffrage as a Safety-Valve.

The Mythical Indispensable Man.

Ignorance as a Medium. — "One can see anything in a fog," is a saying of the Dutch.

On Exchanging Advantages.

Sanscrit for Memoranda.

Responsibility the Basis of Morals.

Applied Christianity.

This World in the Next. — Farrar, in his lecture on Dante.

Living on the Privations of Others.

Living on Brilliant Hopes.

An Enthusiast Without a Mission.

What to Do with the Kittens?

The Fool's Eye in an Old Head.

On Being Found Out. — Fag in The Rivals.

The Fury Passions. — "The vultures of the mind."

The Unforgiving Eye. — Sir Oliver's.

The Dread of Scolding Women. — Captain Cuttle, after he fled from Mrs. MacStinger's, "lived a very close and retired life, seldom stirring abroad after dark; venturing even then only into the obscurest streets, never going forth at all on Sundays; and both within and without the walls of his retreat, avoiding bonnets, as if they were worn by raging lions." Hesiod. Juno's tongue. Doctor to his patient.

The Universal Dependence.

Posthumous Reflections.

Behind the Time, and Poor. — Solomon Gills.

Making an Effort. — Mrs. Chick's reply.

The Desolation of Disuse. — Dombey's house.

Rash Judgment. — One of Lamb's Essays. Wesley's warning.

Sanctified Immoralities.

Books in Phrases. — In Shakespeare, Browne, Sterne, Emerson, etc., and in every wise man's conversation.

The Mystery of the Lady.

Personal Option.

The Goitre of Egotism. — Emerson.

Self-Swindlers.

Difficulties of Decency.

Vice of Rectitude.

Wrath of Celestial Minds.

Congestion of Ideas.

Accident, as Element or Factor. — Napoleon. Wellington. Napier.

Excess in Temperance.

The Hobby Club. — Each member to be permitted uninterrupted opportunity to air his hobby.

The Slow Coach. — A newspaper, to be made up from the papers of the day previous, — the objectionable and the ephemeral to be omitted.

The Eddy of Indecision.

Masks.

The Art of Friendliness.

The Uneasiness of Remorse.

The Loneliness of Pride.

Sailing on a Wish from World to World.

Whatsoever ye would do unto others do ye even so unto them.

Lord be merciful unto him a sinner.

Passions and Aversions. — Fouché.

The Litany of our Little Miseries.

How to make Superfluous People Content?

Homes for the Indolent.

www.ingramcontent.com/pod-product-compliance
Lightning Source LLC
Chambersburg PA
CBHW030009240426
43672CB00007B/886